Blowing the Doors Off!

A Defense Manual for Christian Students

by James Patrick Holding

Blowing the Doors Off!
by James Patrick Holding

Printed in the United States of America

ISBN 978-1-60647-991-9

The King James Version was also used.

www.xulonpress.com

Dedication

For Dr. John Reinhold, whose dream is the inspiration for this book.

For C. M., and Austin Kidder, who made it possible for the book to become a reality.

Table of Contents

Foreword: A Message to Parents

By Sean Yost

Imagine watching thousands of young people headed unknowingly toward the edge of a cliff that will plummet them to their death, yet you are unable to help them or warn them in any way of the danger ahead.

Imagine that you ***are*** equipped with every tool you could possibly need to get their attention and alert them of the impending danger and certain death if they continue along their path toward the cliff.

Now, envision yourself on a typical college campus, watching young Christians searching for their identity—unprepared for the bombardment by skeptical and atheistic worldviews, unable to stand before the onslaught of intellectual cynicism that attacks their faith. How will you, a mature Christian, help them "own their faith?"

It is our responsibility as Christian leaders and parents to help lead this generation down the right path. (Deuteronomy 6:6-9) It is our duty to ensure that they arrive at the next step after high school graduation fully committed to God and completely prepared to resist the culture's invasion to shake their faith. When they leave our youth group, discipleship group, and sanctuary and head into unfamiliar territory, let's make sure they are equipped.

In this defense manual for Christian Students, J.P. Holding has provided a critical tool that will arm this generation to stand strong in the midst of this cultural assault, helping them come out on the other end of their education with a solid faith in Christ that will serve them for eternity.

Blowing the Doors Off!—A Defense Manual for Christian Students—don't let your kids leave home without it!

Sean is Associate Pastor and Director of Family Development at Christ the Redeemer Church - Ponte Vedra Beach, FL, Assistant Bishop for the Redeemer Family of Churches and Ministries, founder and Executive Director of YouthQuake Live and co-host of the TV series The Ultimate Choice. Sean's passion is to see young people established in the purpose and destiny that God has for their individual lives and for their generation.

Laying the Foundation

Let's start with a question that, if we don't answer, you may as well not even bother reading any more: "Why is it that I should read this in the first place? I could be playing with my Xbox instead." (Believe me – I wouldn't mind a few rounds of gaming myself.)

Introduction:

Why Johnny Can't Believe

If you're a Christian student on your way to college (or, depending on where you live, they may call it a "university"), there are all kinds of boring statistics out there that tell us some bad news: There's a real good chance – at least a 50% chance — that by the time you leave college, you won't be calling yourself a Christian any more.

Sure, this doesn't happen to *everyone*, especially if you go to a Christian school. But it happens. We know that as a whole, church attendance, prayer, and Bible reading become less important to students who attend secular colleges or universities, and that many of them won't come back to church as adults, either. (And it doesn't happen just to people who go to college: Even a lot of students who go straight out into the world without college say they're dropping out of Christianity.)

One guy who really looked into this is Dr. Steve Henderson, who used to be vice-president of a place called the Noel Levitz Center for Enrollment Management. (That long name just means, he works for a place where they have plenty of experts on stuff like this.) Basically, Henderson says that when you go off to advanced school, you end up re-examining the values you were taught at home and in church. At times like that you look around for someone who knows what they're talking about and can give some advice, and most of the time, what you find are teachers and professors who are usually not Christians, and actually will be antagonistic towards Christianity and Christian values, as well as other students who are the same way.

This isn't meant to be paranoid – I'm not saying that there are people all over colleges or out in the world "out to get you" and stop you from being a Christian (though I do know **some** people who are like that!). But it is true that college is a place where a lot of new ideas can be discovered, and where there are teachers and professors who are hostile to religion (of all kinds) and would like to change the minds of others. It's also true that even if you skip college, you'll still run into a lot of new and different ideas. Either way, there's a very good chance that your faith will be challenged as it never has been.

Blowing the Doors Off! is designed to help you, as a Christian student or graduate, withstand the assaults on your faith that will always come when attending a secular institution or when you first enter into a new world of ideas that comes along as sure as your drivers' license. I've spent a lot of time dealing with arguments like the ones you'll read here, and I want to make sure that you're aware that when you hear what the doubters have to say, you know that there's another side to the story.

Please keep in mind that this book is only a "starter" for you to get to more detailed answers. That's why I list "recommended reading" all through the book. The answers in this book are just food for thought sometimes – they may not answer all possible arguments, because a book like that wouldn't be that easy to use. (It'd be larger than your dorm room, for example.) So at the end of most chapters, we'll provides Internet links that tell you were to find more, and more detailed, information on the subject of the chapter. We'll also have, at the end of the book, a special bibliography (reading list) of both books and Internet materials you can look up for more information on the topics in this book, and other topics we haven't covered.

Ultimately, whatever I say in this book, only **you** can decide what you believe and what you *want* to believe. All I ask is that you give a fair hearing to the responses made to the critics of Christianity. There's a *lot* of stuff out there that can give us good, solid answers – libraries filled with books that defend what we believe. Be willing to check it out, too, when someone tries to give you reasons to doubt. That's all I ask.

If you have any questions, please feel free to write me at jphold@earthlink.net or contact me at my website at http://www.tektonics.org. I'll have a special page there for people who read this book, and a link to a discussion forum, too (theologyweb.com).

Take care, and God bless,

J. P. Holding

Chapter 1

The Fallacy Collection

LOGICAL
ILLOGICAL
"Live long and prosper."
"Perish quickly in poverty."

Knowing what arguments are true or false means we have to know facts, of course. But more often than not, we also have to know a little more – like how to think about *how* facts are presented. In other words, we have to know how to reason correctly, too.

If you've ever watched the old *Star Trek* show (the real, real old one – with Kirk and McCoy, not Data and Picard) you might remember Mr. Spock. He was a Vulcan, and a Vulcan was always logical – he always knew how to think about facts and use them. He always collected the information he needed first. Then he decided, using his logic, what the best course of action was. Spock was also good at finding the mistakes in other people's arguments (**especially** Dr. McCoy's arguments).

It's always a good idea to be able to find errors in logic, so you can avoid them in *your* arguments. It's also good to be able to detect errors in the reasoning of other people's arguments. The rest of this book will tell you about claims of fact, but in this part, we'll give you some examples of typical mistakes in logic.

Appeal to Authority

Let's face it: Not one person will ever become qualified as an expert in *everything*. You can spend decades studying only one subject alone (that's what happens when you get a Ph. D.). Most people will have to rely on experts from time to time to prove a point, and we ask experts to help us solve problems all the time. When we need help with a sore stomach after eating 500 "nuclear spicy" chicken wings, we talk to a doctor, and we hope he's had a good education in medical school. When your toilet overflows, and the water gets so high that you can do your homework while floating on your chair, you look for an expert in fixing it – a plumber. You don't just open the phone book and call Tire Kingdom because that's where your finger landed.

The point is that appealing to an authority to make a point *can* be an acceptable way to make an argument. But there's a form of arguing that way that *isn't* right, called the Appeal to the Authority.

One way to commit this fallacy is to use a claim from a person who is not qualified to comment on the area you are making the argument in. For example, here is how someone might argue:

> Albert Einstein stated that, "God does not play dice."
>
> *Therefore*, random probability (luck) is in contradiction to God's sovereign plan.

The conclusion may be correct, but the argument is bad because Einstein was an expert in science, not theology. This happens a lot when people appeal to the opinions of celebrities or politicians to make an argument. You may also see it happen when people appeal to a teacher or professor (who may or may not be an expert in a field they're commenting on).

Another kind of appealing to false authority is to say that something is proved right because "many" or "most" authorities say it is. For instance, someone can say, "the majority of scholars think that the historical Jesus was just a really good teacher." This may be true (and it probably is). However, you need to back up this argument by naming an authority that says it.

Finally, we have to keep in mind that many authorities can be very qualified in the same field and still contradict one another. In that case, we may need to look at the arguments from both sides more closely to see if maybe one authority knows more than the other, or if one authority is making a mistake in logic that the other does not.

Begging the Question (a.k.a. Circular Reasoning)

Circular reasoning happens when the conclusion of an argument is contained in one of its premises. An example:

1) The Gospels contain several prophecies of the Fall of Jerusalem and the destruction of the Temple.
2) Any supposed prophecy of an event that actually occurred was probably written in hindsight.
3) The Romans attacked and destroyed Jerusalem (including the Temple) in 70 A.D. (i.e. Mat 23:37, 38; Mark 13:1-3).
4) *Therefore*, the Gospels were probably written after 70 A.D.

The argument begs the question because premise 2 contains a conclusion hidden inside it. Premise 2 can't just be assumed – the person has to prove by argument that real prophecy can't happen.

Cause and Effect Fallacy (a.k.a. Questionable Cause)

Did you know that cold weather causes illness? Or that the rise in Christianity in the last couple of decades caused the rise of immorality in society? Believe it or not, many people do believe the former (rather, bacteria and viruses cause illness), and I really have seen a Skeptic assert the second. (Of course, the rise of immorality in American society has many complex causes, and it is likely that the rise of Christianity is coincidence.)

These two claims are cause-and-effect fallacies. If event B occurs just after event A or simultaneously, it is a fallacy to jump to the conclusion that A causes B. Several possibilities exist:

- A and B may just happen to occur together (coincidence). Neither is the cause of the other.
- A and B may both be caused by another event, C.
- Maybe A did cause B, but such that has to be proven with evidence, not just argued.

For example:

1. One of the Protestant movement's most important doctrines is *Sola Scriptura* (Scripture alone).
2. The Protestant denominations have since broken up.
3. *Therefore, Sola Scriptura* causes denominational splitting.

This argument is a fallacy because no evidence is shown here that *Sola Scriptura* does cause denominational splitting. I could likewise suppose that denominational splitting causes *Sola Scriptura*, or that both have a common cause, or that it is just coincidence. Unless the person making this argument has the historical evidence to support that cause and effect reasoning, the argument is no good.

Equivocation

The Fallacy of Equivocation happens when a word is used in two different contexts and is assumed to have the same meaning in both contexts, when different meanings ought to be used. Two examples:

1) All bushes are green and leafy.
2) *Therefore*, George W. Bush is green and leafy.

Or:

1) Isaiah 44:6 says, "Thus says the LORD, the King of Israel and his Redeemer, the LORD of hosts: 'I am the first and I am the last, And there is no God [*elohim*] besides Me."
2) Psalm 82 implies there are many gods [*elohim*]. (*Ye are gods...*)
3) *Therefore*, Isaiah and Psalms contradict one another.

The second example assumes that *elohim* has the same meaning in both passages. In reality, Isaiah 44:6 most likely refers to what we would call deity (gods), whereas Psalm 82 either refers to angels or more likely the leadership of Israel. The Hebrew term *elohim* can refer to *Yahweh* (God), deity, or beings of power. (See the chapter, "How Many Es in Elohim?" By the way, the Fallacy of Equivocation is often committed by critics of the Bible because they don't realize that ancient languages only had a few thousand words each, unlike modern languages like English, which can have over a million words. Sometimes words had to do "extra duty" with more than one meaning.)

False Dilemma

A False Dilemma is one in which only two answers are proposed, when a third or more might be available. An example:

> Either you accept Naturalism (the idea that miracles never happen and that there is not such thing as a spiritual world), or you are superstitious.

In this case, it is assumed that the only alternative to the philosophy of Naturalism is superstition. It doesn't even allow for a well-thought-out and evidenced belief in God or in miracles.

Guilt By Association

"I can't believe you are a Christian! ______ *was a Christian!*" This is a real argument I have seen used, and while most critics won't use it, you still see it from time to time. Some bad person's name is put in the blank – someone like Hitler or Stalin, or maybe someone like a televangelist who steals money from people, or someone like Ted Haggard who committed some obnoxious sin.

The point here is not whether Hitler or Haggard were or were not Christian. The point is that this is an example of a fallacy known as Guilt By Association. In its most common form, this fallacy attempts to make someone or some idea look bad by associating it with a bad person or a group. This argument can be easily reversed and shown to be a fallacy. We could fill in the blank with a very good person's name instead (like Billy Graham). Or we could find examples of very noble causes that have attracted some shady characters.

Genetic Fallacy

A Genetic Fallacy happens when the origin of a belief or idea is presented as a reason to accept or reject the idea. This is a common example of a genetic fallacy:

> Most Christians are believers because their parents were.

Typically, though not always, the hidden conclusion is "therefore Christianity is not true." But this only tells how and why people believe something – not whether what they believe is true.

Hasty Generalization

The Hasty Generalization is a way of jumping to a conclusion with a limited amount of information. The most common kinds of Hasty Generalization are *stereotypes*, which are overly broad generalizations of certain types of people. For example:

Some of the Christians I met are hypocritical.

Therefore, all Christians are hypocrites.

Certain types of generalization *can* be right, but we have to have enough information to justify it. For example, if we see 100 ravens and they are all black, it is reasonable to conclude that all ravens will be black. But we still need to be careful, because maybe someday we will see albino ravens.

Loaded Question

"Have you stopped beating your wife?" This is an old joke, but it is an example of a loaded question. A loaded question is a question phrased so that it forces an answer based on a false or controversial assumption. It is *assumed* in the question that I beat my wife – the question is formed to permit only a "yes" or "no" answer, but not an answer that means I have *never* beaten my wife (though you can always explain that).

If you don't give an answer to a loaded question but instead point out that it is loaded, sometimes you are accused of dodging it. Though many times a loaded question is raised unintentionally, it is a common tactic to trap a person into agreeing with a questionable claim, or to accuse them of "dodging an important issue."

Appeal to Popularity (a.k.a. Bandwagon Fallacy)

An appeal to popularity is sort of like the argument from authority, except the appeal is not to what kind of person agrees with the claim, but how many people agree with it. For example:

> The majority of people in the world think Jesus really existed.
>
> *Therefore*, Jesus really existed.

Once again, the conclusion may be true, but the reason for believing the conclusion is not good enough.

Quoting Out of Context

Quoting out of context may be one of the most important fallacies for readers of this book. Far too often the Bible is quoted out of context, creating a supposed contradiction or a doctrine made up on the spot.

Context usually is a key ingredient in the meaning of a quote. To be sure, not every instance of quoting out of context is seriously fallacious; sometimes it is better to be brief. However, we should always be careful not to change the meaning too much.

For example, there was once a woman who had a really dim view of life, and she never enjoyed anything. She wouldn't eat good foods, or go to movies, or do anything fun. When she was asked why she didn't do this, she quoted Colossians 2:21:

> Do not handle, do not taste, do not touch!

She took this verse out of context to forbid all experience of enjoyment. When we read the passage this is in, we see:

> If you have died with Christ to the elementary principles of the world, why, as if you were living in the world, do you submit yourself to decrees, such as, "Do not handle, do not taste, do not touch!" (which all refer to things destined to perish with use) — in accordance with the commandments and teachings of men? These are matters which have, to be sure, the appearance of wisdom in self-made religion and self-abasement and severe treatment of the body, but are of no value against fleshly indulgence. Colossians 2:20-23.

Here, Paul is not unpacking some deep truth about not enjoying life, but instead is refuting a mistake. "Do not handle, do not taste, do not touch," was a slogan that Paul was refuting, not advice he was giving to everyone. (He was probably refuting a type of heretic who thought the body was evil – later on these became people we now call the *Gnostics*. The Gnostics would have never gone to movies.) That means that the woman was incorrectly quoting out of context in her use of Col. 2:21.

Red Herring

A red herring isn't a fish – it is an irrelevant topic or claim brought into a discussion to distract you from the topic being discussed. You might also say it is changing the subject. Here's an example:

> Person A: We must support the war in Slobovia, because we have to finish what we started.
>
> Person B: I would support the President with the war in Slobovia, but I don't like his policy on the economy.

Person B has changed the subject from the war in Slobovia to the economy.

Slippery Slope

The slippery slope is a fallacy that asserts the result of some event without explaining how the result follows from the event. For instance:

> If we allow creationism to be taught in public schools as an alternative to evolution, then next thing you know, they will teach a flat earth and a solid sky as an alternative to modern cosmology.
>
> If they restrict pornography today, tomorrow they will take away all of your freedom of speech.

If there was some reasoning that tells us how flat-earth-solid-sky teaching follows from teaching creationism or how loss of all freedom of speech follows from restricting porn, these examples would not commit the slippery slope fallacy.

Special Pleading

Special pleading happens when a person holds others to a different standard, without any good reason. For example, a critic may ask a Christian to prove that Jesus existed. When the Christian asks the critic to prove his case that Jesus did not exist, the critic can't just say, "the burden of proof is on you." They must provide a reason why their belief is valid, or explain why the burden of proof is on the Christian. Just saying it is, doesn't shift the burden.

Those are just a few of the logical fallacies you might see running around out there – so when you go out to debate people, make sure you can spot these. Either that, or see if you can get Mr. Spock to be there, too!

Read More!

<http://www.tektonics.org/guest/fallacies.html>

This article gives a much longer list of fallacies and even more examples of them. It was originally written by Justin Moser, and inspired this chapter.

Chapter 2:

The Abomination That Causes Misinformation

I'll bet a lot of you use the online encyclopedia called "Wikipedia" when you need to know stuff. I'll also bet you have a lot of teachers who tell you *not* to use is as a source when you write a report. Right?

There's a lot of good reasons for that. The main one is that Wikipedia is something anyone can log on to and change to say whatever they want. And sure, the people who run it say that they try to make sure the information is accurate, but let's face it – they can't be everywhere at once, and it is a big, big, BIG website. They're also not experts themselves. That's why I don't give much respect to people who try to argue with me and use Wikipedia for their information (and also why I call Wikipedia "the abomination that causes misinformation"!).

But maybe you're asking me, okay, if *you're* so smart, how do *you* find out stuff? What can you do when you have two or more different sources that say two different things? How can you decide which is true? How can you tell whether a book or website or whatever is a good source of information and whether what it says deserves to be listened to?

The answer many people give is, "You can't. Let's throw up our hands and go watch the Super Bowl." Others say, "Just pick who you like best." The real answer is more complicated: **You follow some basic research guidelines.** Understand that none of these guidelines is a 100%, ironclad, no-exceptions absolute – but the fewer of these rules are met, the less likely it is that the source you have is worth using.

1. **Check their credentials!** This one is so important it needs to be beaten into the ground, and then when it is done, it needs to be beaten some more and some more. Most

books will have some kind of short biography giving a person's credentials. It should tell you what their education has been, give a highlight of publishing credits (you can look for someone's "vitae" or resume' if you want a **full** list; with many scholars, they won't fit on a book's cover or flyleaf), and maybe name some scholarly groups they belong to (such as the Society for Biblical Literature). If these are either:

a. **Missing** (the publisher may not have had room, or if your book is missing a paper cover, it may have been there — but other than that...)
b. **Not relevant** (i.e., a book on Biblical scholarship written by someone with a Ph. D. in aerodynamics! – like we said before, when you have a sick stomach, you don't see a plumber, you see a doctor!)
c. **Unclear** (i.e., it says they "got a Ph. D. at Vanderbilt" but does not say in **what**)

....you'll need to think about that source a bit. Obviously such credentials are not required to be right in what you argue (especially if you *use* sources with credentials to write a book) but they can help you decide whether an author is likely to have credibility and be telling the truth.

2. **Check their sources.** A respectable source should have some sort of bibliography and/or notes. Look at these carefully. Warning signs on this are:
    a. If you see **the same sources used over and over.** This could indicate someone who hasn't done a lot of work themselves and is just copying other people without understanding the subject. Of course you'll need to consider other possibilities (is the author offering a refutation of or "update" to the source he uses?), but re-use of the same sources over and over again is often a danger sign.
    b. If you see **incomplete citations or none at all** — if the source has no notes (just a bibliography), or bad ones, they likely don't know what they're talking about. Though be careful: You don't need a note for an obvious claim like, "the sky is blue" and many scholars will not need a note for something that is that obvious in their field of knowledge.
    c. If you see sources **that are really old** — unless the book is a review of history or something like that, high use of sources that aren't recent could be a sign of someone not doing good research.

d. Finally, watch out for "**padding**" – listing sources in a bibliography that are not actually used, or are used only a little. (Your teachers know about this, and they don't like it either!)

3. **Any recommendations?** These days a good source may have recommendations from other writers or from review publications on their cover. These can be good to check. If good comments come from a fairly broad spectrum of people with different beliefs (in other words, not just from people who agree with the author on many things, but also disagree with them on some things) you're likely in good shape. Recommends from just people who believe like they do are not as good but can still be worthwhile. Recommends from nobodies or from people who are not experts (like, say, Britney Spears!) don't help a bit.
4. **Reviews.** If you want to dig deep, check for reviews of the book in what are called *peer-reviewed* publications (that is, magazines by people who are experts) or in general reviewing sources like *Publishers Weekly*. Watch out though, because some books will just quote the favorable part of a review on their cover and ignore the parts where the review points out flaws.
5. **And what's not a good reason to prefer a source?** It's sad to have to say this, but since people do think these are reasons a source is or is not credible, they have to be mentioned:

V. **"It's biased towards a point of view."** That may be true, but it may be true for a good reason. Every source is "biased" to a point of view, and the truth is always biased.

A. **"It's published by a fundamentalist/atheist/cultic press."** This *sometimes* gives critical information about a writer, but not always. The way it is used, it is a Genetic Fallacy (see the chapter before this one).

B. **"It's a best seller!"** So was *Mein Kampf* in pre-Nazi Germany! (Go back and look in the last chapter at what it says about an "Appeal to Popularity.")

C. **"It's provocative/it opens your mind!"** An open mind is a good thing until a person's brains fall out! It is something you close once you find the truth. It's more important that something tell the truth than that it "provokes" thought (the thoughts it "provokes" may be wrong).

Once again, these are just some general guidelines; they are far from ironclad, and they are certainly no substitute for logical and critical thinking. In fact, you really can't use one without the other. Have fun!

Chapter 3:

How the Bible Talks To You

It may be hard to believe if you read the King James Version, but it is true: The people who lived in the time of the Bible didn't speak modern English. It seems strange to have to say that, but some critics of the Bible actually argue as though they did (or else, they say that God could have made things more clear to them by having people in Bible times speak in modern English).

For example, critics often attack the Bible for using what is called *exclusive language*: Words like, "all", "none", or "utterly." They point to passages that use these words, and then say that there are exceptions to the "all", etc. and so the Bible is wrong. Here's one I've seen many times (I'll use the King James Version for this one, because that's what most people use when they bring this up):

> 1 Samuel 15:8 And he took Agag the king of the Amalekites alive, and utterly destroyed all the people with the edge of the sword.

They'll then look further on in 1 Samuel, and see how the Amalekites were still around, and say, "Hey, I thought the Amalekites were 'utterly destroyed' and now here they come back making trouble just a few chapters later. What were they, Zombie Amalekites? Ha ha!" No, we just need to understand the way ancient people talked. Compare that verse in 1 Samuel to this inscription offered by the Egyptian Pharaoh Ramesses III:

> I slew the Denyon in their islands, while the Tjekker and Philistines were made ashes. The Sherden and the Washesh of the sea were made non-existent, captured all together and

> brought on captivity to Egypt like the sands of the shore.

Now when Ramesses tells us his enemies were "made non-existent," he was not meaning this literally, since he goes on to say that they were captured. This is just like 1 Samuel 15:8 – it isn't meant to be literal. It's like football fans who celebrate a team's win by shouting, "We're #1!" — even if the team has lost more games than it has won. (Kind of like the Miami Dolphins lately…ugh.)

The people of the Bible had what some scholars call a *dramatic orientation.* They liked to make their speech and writing interesting rather than just saying what happened in a simple, boring way. Here's another example that comes from someone from a similar culture. What would you do if you went to visit a friend, and they said:

> "You have extremely honored me by coming into my abode. I am not worthy of it. This house is yours; you may burn it if you wish. My children are also at your disposal; I would sacrifice them all for your pleasure."

You'd probably be shocked and offended, and want to call the police right away. But what this person is really saying is no more than "I am delighted to see you; please make yourself at home." He's not expecting you to literally ask him to kill his family and burn his house down.

Another example from the Bible is Luke 14:26 (I'll use the NIV this time):

> If anyone comes to me and does not **hate** his father and mother, his wife and children, his brothers and sisters—yes, even his own life—he cannot be my disciple.

Critics can't believe Jesus wanted people to literally *hate* their families! And they're right – we should read this as "love less". This is a typical example of how people in the Bible's culture used a strong word to emphasize what they were saying.

There's another sort of literature in the Bible that critics also sometimes read incorrectly, and that is *proverbial* literature. The book of Proverbs (of course!) is the best example of this, but proverbial material is also found in other parts of the Bible, even in the sayings of Jesus.

Proverbs were supposed to be short and easily memorized. This means it is not expected to be right in what it says in all possible circumstances. It is like advice, not an absolute that is always true all the time. Critics may think they can find mistakes in the Bible by finding exceptions to proverbs. For example, Ecclesiastes 1:9 says "there is nothing new under the sun." I know of a critic who said that was wrong because when America landed on the moon, that was new! But you can do the same thing to modern proverbs too and claim they are "wrong." For example:

1. "He who hesitates is lost." This proverb is saying that that quick action leads to success, while self-doubt means disaster. Obviously this is not always true: Self-doubt may lead to preservation sometimes – like when you use a chainsaw!
2. "Practice makes perfect." Does it always? Obviously not, because sometimes people don't have the talent to become perfect at something they try, or even come close (like the guys in *Dumb and Dumber*).
3. "Poets are born, not made." You can substitute anything for "poets" here — the point is that education cannot replace skill. Not only is this obviously not absolutely true, it contradicts "practice makes perfect" if both are taken absolutely!

The bottom line: The Bible has to be read in the way its writers intended, not as *we* intend it!

Read More!

<http://www.tektonics.org/gk/hyperbole.html>
<http://www.tektonics.org/lp/proverbiallit.html>

These two articles will give you more insight into the use of language in the Bible. Be sure and also check out some of the books we'll list in the Reading Room.

Chapter 4

Culture Shock!

Have you ever met a person from another, very different culture than America's? Maybe you have friends from Japan, or China, or Africa. Maybe you've even been invited to their house for dinner.

If you have, you've probably noticed that their way of thinking about things is different than someone who has lived in America all their life. Today, when we try to appreciate other people's cultures, it becomes important to be aware of and sensitive to cultural differences. For example, if your host is from Japan, you may take your shoes off before entering their home, even though you would never do that when entering your house.

Think of the Bible as someone else's house. Paul, Peter, and John, were not Americans.

They had their own culture and way of thinking, and there are times when we can understand the Bible better by knowing what their culture was like. Let's look at a few important examples.

Honor and Shame

What do we mean by "honor"? *Honor* means that other people think well of you. The opposite word, *shame*, means people think badly of you. In America, we don't always care what other people think of us, but in the majority of cultures, what other people think of you is very, very important. In Japan, for example, people will sometimes kill themselves when they are very ashamed.

The Bible's world was one in which honor was very important to people. And one of the ways this affects our understanding of Christianity is when we realize that crucifixion – the way Jesus died – was considered the most shameful (not-honorable) way for a person to die. When we see Jesus on the cross, we may feel sorry for him, but people who lived in his time would have simply been disgusted, and felt no sympathy. This is one reason why the Resurrection had to happen: It was a way to restore honor to Jesus (and show that God was on his side, and not on the side of those who put him to death). It also tells us that people back then would have had a very hard time believing in Christianity unless there was proof that the resurrection happened.

Where You're From

Today it is considered rude to make fun of someone because they come from a certain part of the country, or because they are from a certain culture. However, in the time of the Bible, what we would call *prejudices* and *stereotypes* were accepted as the truth, even by people who were members of the group being described.

This is important to understand because Jesus himself had "three strikes" against him based on where he was from. He was from Judaea, and most people in the Roman world didn't like Jewish people. He was also from Galilee, a place that people thought was full of rebels. (It would be like saying someone was from "Afghanistan" today – they were associated with political rebellion and terrorism.) He was also from Nazareth, which was a very small town – and people from small towns were thought to not amount to much.

It would have been very hard to preach a crucified savior, but even harder to preach one that came from the worst possible place!

What's New?

People today are always on the lookout for anything new and exciting. People of the world of the Bible were, too – because they wanted to be sure and avoid it! For the people of the Bible, old was good and new was bad. "Always, everywhere, by everyone!" was a motto of first century Roman people. But Christianity said, "Not now, not here, and not you!" And it was *especially* bad when you tried to bring in new religious ideas. That made it hard on Christianity – in fact, it made Christians look like rebels and subversives (like many people look at guys who dye their hair pink).

Group Identity

Have you ever heard someone say that they "didn't know who they were"? In the ancient world, people answered that question in a simple way – they asked other people who they were, and then followed what other people said. Each person had certain role expectations they were expected to fulfill.

But Christianity said NO to that idea. It said that there was neither male nor female, neither rich nor poor, neither slave nor free, in Christ Jesus. Christians said that the whole classification scheme people depended on to know what they were expected to do, didn't matter any more.

What this means is that someone like Jesus needed the support and endorsement of others to support his claims of identity. A person like Jesus could not have kept a ministry going unless those around him supported him. A merely human Jesus who couldn't do miracles, could not have met this demand and must have provided convincing proofs of his power and authority to maintain a following, and for a movement to have started and survived well beyond him. A merely human Jesus would have had to live up to the expectations of others and would have been abandoned at the first sign of failure.

No Privacy

Do you value your privacy? Do you like to be able to be alone? Then don't move to the world of the Bible. In cultures like the one in Bible times, people were always being nosy and minding other people's business. Strangers were viewed as a threat because no one knew what to expect from them; so they were always checked out thoroughly. This means that Christianity would have had a hard time unless it had had convincing proof that Jesus rose from the dead. Missionaries would have been checked out and closely questioned. People hearing the Gospel message would check against the facts — especially where a movement with a radical message like Christianity was concerned. The empty tomb *would* be checked. Matthew's story of resurrected saints would be checked out. Lazarus would be sought out for questioning. Excessive honor claims, such as that Jesus had been resurrected, or his claims to be divine, would have been looked at closely. And later, new Christians would have to answer to their neighbors. If the Pharisees checked Jesus on things like washing his hands and grain picking, and if large crowds gathered around Jesus each time he so much as sneezed — how much more would things like a claimed resurrection have been looked at!

Read More!

<http://www.tektonics.org/lp/nowayjose.html>

Chapter 5:

Christian Myths

It's not a secret: *Some Christians believe things that are wrong.*

Some of the things you'll see me list below you may agree with. Other things may surprise you. Most of them we'll talk about in later chapters, so that this chapter will (hopefully!) make you want to read more. But these are all things a lot of Christians believe, and sometimes, they become "roadblocks" for people to believe or to keep believing. And maybe, if we "bust" some of these myths, it can help you or someone else believe more, or more strongly.

(Okay, I'm not Jamie or Adam, but I do have a job busting myths like they do!)

Hell is a place of physical torture. This myth has caused many people to question the fairness and justness of God. It is grist for many atheist critiques. While I once defended this view myself, and while I do not necessarily think atheist critiques of the idea are sound, there is certainly no reason to make things harder on ourselves and others.

Hell is actually more of a state than a place, and it is a state of shame, of exclusion from God's honor and presence, not a place of torture. See the chapter titled "What in Hell?" for more information.

God is my buddy, Jesus is my friend. I have to define something here. By "friend" I mean like, someone you can sit down and watch TV with. A lot of Christians today have this idea that God and Jesus are their buddies. (A new book called *The Shack* is like this.) Yes, Jesus calls his disciples "friends" in the Gospel of John, but in that time and culture, a "friend" was someone who looked out for your practical interests — not someone you watched football with.

There are many mistakes that follow this one. Some Christians see God as a "sugar daddy" who passes out wealth like a slot machine, and whose voice is constantly in one's head, sometimes contradicting sound practice and doctrine, but sometimes even just giving advice on what house or car to buy.

Many Christians speak of a "personal relationship with Jesus". I would rather hear people say that what is required of us is a *patronal* relationship with Jesus. The Bible describes our relationship with God in a way that is like what we now call a *client-patron relationship*, one in which God, a patron, is remote; and Jesus, as a broker, mediates (acts as a go-between) between ourselves and God. (The indwelling Holy Spirit acts as a broker too in this.)

Faith is blind and has nothing to do with evidence. Not so! Faith in fact means loyalty based on prior performance. See the chapter, "Bible Dictionary."

Heaven is a place to relax. This idea has led some Christians to think Heaven will be a boring place. Not at all. See the chapter, "What in Heaven?"

Certainty is a sin. This myth holds that everyone's opinion is valid and deserves "respect" and/or wider hearing. This is not only non-Biblical (for those who respect that authority) but also self-contradictory, because it fails to respect the "opinion" that not everyone's opinion is valid. "Tolerance" that doesn't allow for the idea that it is in error in being tolerant, is *in*tolerant.

Sanitized for your protection. Modern versions of the Bible, and everyday preachers, have often failed to deal with "hard sayings" of the Bible, whether it be language that we would call objectionable (Malachi's "dung in your faces" phrase, etc.) or behavior that we would regard as immoral (the destruction of the Amalekites, etc.) Then when Christians discover these passages in the Bible, they are shocked by them and have no idea how to defend or explain them. That's one of the myths we hope to bust with this book and the sources listed in it.

"Love" means good feelings. The Biblical word for "love"(*agape*) does not refer to good feelings, but to looking out for the greater good. See again the chapter, "Bible Dictionary."

Old Testament prophecy fulfillment is a good proof of Christianity. We've made a mistake by pointing to Old Testament "predictions" of Jesus in many cases. Most of these are not "predictions" (a few are). It is not so much that the OT predicted the NT events, as that the NT writers looked at history and then looked for OT passages that echoed what they had seen. This is why the NT allegedly uses OT passages "out of context" as some critics say. It doesn't. See more in the chapter, "Fictional Friction."

A church is a building. The ancient word *ekklesia* which is translated "church" meant the people and the assembly of people, not where they met. The same goes for the Jewish synagogue (which required ten men, not ten bricks). This myth has often taken the focus away from the body of Christ where it belongs and put it on things and programs where it doesn't belong. It also encourages a view of people as statistics.

The supernatural exists. Uh oh, what am I saying? Don't panic: I'm saying that we've all fallen for a false distinction between the natural and the so-called supernatural. This has led to ideas that miracles (acts of God) "violate natural law". See the Chapter, "God Breaks the Law."

The Old Testament

Okay, now it's time to talk about the Bible. We'll start with the Old Testament – makes sense, right, since it comes first? Well, if not, you can always skip around in this book if you want.

Chapter 6:

Babylon One

Have you ever heard of a story called Enuma Elish? You won't find it at Waldenbooks on the bestseller rack, though it may have been back in 1800 BC. (Back then, the store would have been called "Waldenstonetablets.")

Enuma Elish was written by the ancient Babylonians. It's a story of how the world was created, sort of like Genesis. But different. That's important, because some people like to say that the author of Genesis stole a lot of what he wrote from Enuma Elish. But once you read both of them, it's like saying Billy Graham stole his sermons from Elmer Fudd. We'll be quoting lines from Genesis and lines from Enuma Elish so you can compare them and see for yourself.

Most of Enuma Elish is about a battle between the god Marduk (the "creator") and Tiamat the water-goddess. Tiamat ends up being beaten and her body is used to make the universe. Believe it or not, some people think *this* story is basically the same as **this** one:

> Genesis 1:2 Now the earth was formless and empty, darkness was over the surface of the deep, and the Spirit of God was hovering over the waters.

The word for "deep" here is the Hebrew word *tehowm*, and some think this is similar to "Tiamat" and see a connection: Tiamat was the water goddess; *tehowm* is deep water. Sounds the same! Must be a connection, right? You say *Tehomato*, I say **Tiamato**!

But if there's any connection, it would have to show that Enuma Elish borrowed from Genesis, or that both stories came up without influence from the other. Tiamat was only one of *two* water-deities involved in the story. The other was the water-god Apsu. Tiamat was salty water; Apsu was fresh water. There's no parallel to Apsu in Genesis.

More importantly, language experts on Hebrew say there's no way *tehowm* could have come from Tiamat. Hebrew was a language that had "gender" in its words, like German does (but English doesn't). The Hebrew *tehowm* has a masculine ending. *Tiamat* is feminine. A word the came from Babylonian to Hebrew would stay feminine. The word would not be *tehowm* but *tiama* or *teama*. Hebrew would also not add the *H* unless it were found in the original word (it would have to have been *Tihamat*).

> 1:3-5 And God said, "Let there be light," and there was light. God saw that the light was good, and He separated the light from the darkness. God called the light "day," and the darkness he called "night." And there was evening, and there was morning—the first day.

Both Enuma Elish and Genesis say that light was around even before the creation of the sun and moon. But in Enuma Elish, the light *came from* a god ("Apsu harkened unto him and his countenance grew bright"), while in Genesis, it was *created by* God.

> 1:6-10 And God said, "Let there be an expanse between the waters to separate water from water." So God made the expanse and separated the water under the expanse from the water above it. And it was so. God called the expanse "sky." And there was evening, and there was morning—the second day. And God said, "Let the water under the sky be gathered to one place, and let dry ground appear." And it was so. God called the dry ground "land," and the gathered waters he called "seas." And God saw that it was good.

Both Enuma Elish and Genesis report the dividing of two substances. But so do creation accounts from other cultures, such as from Egypt, Phoenicia, and India. It makes better sense to say they were all reporting something from common source (like maybe even real history!) than to say that Genesis borrowed from Enuma Elish.

> 1:11 Then God said, "Let the land produce vegetation: seed-bearing plants and trees on the land that bear fruit with seed in it, according to their various kinds." And it was so.

Here's a big difference. Enuma Elish doesn't report the creation of animals or plants. It may have been in a part of Enuma Elish that was lost, but there wouldn't be much room for it.

> 1:14-18 And God said, "Let there be lights in the expanse of the sky to separate the day from the night, and let them serve as signs to mark seasons and days and years, and let them be lights in the expanse of the sky to give light on the earth." And it was so. God made two great lights—the greater light to govern the day and the lesser light to govern the night. He also made the stars. God set them in the expanse of the sky to give light on the earth, to govern the day and the night, and to separate light from darkness. And God saw that it was good.

> He (Marduk) made the stations for the great gods;
> The stars, their images, as the stars of the Zodiac, he fixed.

> He ordained the year and into sections he divided it;
> For the twelve months he fixed three stars.
> After he had ... the days of the year ... images,
> He founded the station of Nibir [the planet Jupiter] to determine their bounds;
> That none might err or go astray,
> He set the station of Bel and Ea along with him.
> He opened great gates on both sides,
> He made strong the bolt on the left and on the right.
> In the midst thereof he fixed the zenith;
> The Moon-god he caused to shine forth, the night he entrusted to him.
> He appointed him, a being of the night, to determine the days;

Both Enuma Elish and Genesis record the creation of the sun and moon. Both say that they were for light and for keeping time, but that makes sense because all cultures worldwide use the sun and moon for the same purpose. Enuma Elish, though, makes a special point of the creation of the zodiac, which reflects how the Babylonians made a big deal about astrology. Enuma Elish also refers to gates at the east and the west of the sky through which the sun and moon pass (though this could be a metaphor).

> 1:26-30 Then God said, "Let us make man in our image, in our likeness, and let them rule over the fish of the sea and the birds of the air, over the livestock, over all the earth, and over

all the creatures that move along the ground." So God created man in his own image, in the image of God he created him; male and female he created them. God blessed them and said to them, "Be fruitful and increase in number; fill the earth and subdue it. Rule over the fish of the sea and the birds of the air and over every living creature that moves on the ground." Then God said, "I give you every seed-bearing plant on the face of the whole earth and every tree that has fruit with seed in it. They will be yours for food. And to all the beasts of the earth and all the birds of the air and all the creatures that move on the ground—everything that has the breath of life in it—I give every green plant for food." And it was so.

When Marduk heard the words of the gods,
His heart prompted him to fashion artful works.
Opening his mouth, he addressed Ea
To impart the plan he had conceived in his heart:
"I will take blood and fashion bone.
I will establish a savage, 'man' shall be his name.
truly, savage-man I will create.
He shall be charged with the service of the gods
That they might be at ease!
The ways of the gods I will artfully alter…

To Lugaldimmerankia, counselor of the gods, their lord:

"It was Kingu who contrived the uprising,
And made Tiamat rebel, and joined battle."

They bound him, holding him before Ea.
They imposed on him his punishment and
severed his blood vessels.
Out of his blood they fashioned mankind.

Both stories have some of the same things in them at this point. In Genesis, God creates man from dust, and gives him life with His breath or spirit. In Enuma Elish, Marduk gives Ea (another god) a plan to create man, leading Ea to go and kill Kingu (another god) and mix his blood with dirt to make man.

A bigger difference has to do with man's *purpose*. In the Enuma Elish, man is created because Marduk was prompted in his heart to "create ingenious things." Man was like an ego trip for Marduk! Once that is done, man's purpose is to serve the gods, build their temples, and make sacrifices to them. Men are the gods' boot-polishers. But in Genesis, man is not a servant to God. He is God's agent.

Genesis 2:2-3 And on the seventh day God ended his work which he had made; and he rested on the seventh day from all his work which he had made. And God blessed the seventh day, and sanctified it: because that in it he had rested from all his work which God created and made.

Asaru [Marduk], bestower of cultivation, who established water levels;
Creator of grain and herbs, who causes vegetation to sprout.
Asarualim, who is honored in the place of counsel, who excels in counsel;
To whom the gods hope, not being possessed of fear.
Asarualimnunna, the gracious, light of the father, his begetter,
Who directs the decrees of Anu, Enlil, Ea and Ninigiku.
He is their provider who assigns their portions,
Whose horned cap is plenty, multiplying . . . .
Tutu is he, who created then anew.
Let him purify their shrines that they may have ease.
Let him devise the spell that the gods may be at rest.

The gods of the Enuma Elish "rested," sort of — they threw a big party, one that takes up almost two tablets of the Enuma Elish out of seven. By the way, there's no connection between Genesis' 7 *days* and the Enuma Elish's 7 *tablets*. The creation part takes up only four of Enuma Elish's tablets, and it doesn't lay out a seven-day pattern of creation.

So in conclusion, there's really no case to say that Genesis borrowed from Enuma Elish. There are too many wild differences, so that it would be like comparing a play of William Shakespeare to an episode of *Dragonball Z!*

Read More!

<http://www.tektonics.org/af/babgenesis.html>

Chapter 7:

Creation, Times Two

The first two chapters of Genesis are regularly bashed on the head for being contrary to modern science; but we won't be discussing that here. Instead, we're going to look at the claim that there are two "creation accounts" – the first being Genesis 1:1-2:3, and the second being the rest of Genesis 2 – that contradict each other. We'll call these two passages G1 and G2, and we'll use the King James Version for this one because this is what is used when critics make these arguments.

Critics find two major points of disagreement between G1 and G2. The first one is easy to dispose of:

> Gen. 1:11 And God said, Let the earth bring forth grass, the herb yielding seed, and the fruit tree yielding fruit after his kind, whose seed is in itself, upon the earth: and it was so.

Gen. 2:4-5 These are the generations of the heavens and of the earth when they were created, in the day that the LORD God made the earth and the heavens, And every plant of the field before it was in the earth, and every herb of the field before it grew: for the LORD God had not caused it to rain upon the earth, and there was not a man to till the ground.

The claim is that G1 has plants made before man, while G2 has man made before plants. But G2 doesn't say this; it says that what did not exist yet were plants and herbs "of the field" — *what* field? The Hebrew word here is *sadeh*, and it means a limited area of land, or a flat place suitable for agriculture. Notice that verse 2:5 goes on to explain *why* there were no "plants of the field" — because a) there was no rain upon the earth, and b) there was no man to work the earth — the two things needed for *agriculture.* So, what this passage indicates is that there was as yet no organized agriculture, and that makes sense of the verses following, where God specifically plants the Garden of Eden and places man to tend to it. G2 is not indicating that there were no plants created yet **at all**, but that a special place was set aside for the foundation of agriculture and for plants "of the field" to be developed. Sort of like a special greenhouse (but without the roof).

Gen. 1:24-5 And God said, Let the earth bring forth the living creature after his kind, cattle, and creeping thing, and beast of the earth after his kind: and it was so. And God made the beast of the earth after his kind, and cattle after their kind, and every thing that creepeth upon the earth after his kind: and God saw that it was good.

Gen. 2:18-20 And the LORD God said, It is not good that the man should be alone; I will make him an help meet for him. And out of the ground the LORD God formed every beast of the field, and every fowl of the air; and brought them unto Adam to see what he would call them: and whatsoever Adam called every living creature, that was the name thereof. And Adam gave names to all cattle, and to the fowl of the air, and to every beast of the field; but for Adam there was not found an help meet for him.

G1 says that animals were created before man; G2 says that man came first, there was a need to designate a helpmeet, and then animals were created for the first time...or does it? For quite some time now the most used solution to this problem has been to do what the New International Version of the Bible does, and that is to render the verb in verse 2:19 not as simple past tense, but as what is called a *pluperfect*, so:

Now the LORD God **had formed** out of the ground all the beasts of the field and all the birds of the air.

Some Hebrew scholars agree with the way this is translated, and the arguments for it are good enough to keep. But if someone wants to argue, there's another answer.

The naming of the animals by Adam wasn't just for making nametags. It was a demonstration of Adam's authority over the entirety of nature. In Bible times, the giving of names was an exercise showing who was in charge.

Now let's look at Gen. 2:18-20 again, only this time we'll highlight some words:

> And the LORD God said, It is not good that the man should be alone; I will make him an help meet for him. And out of the ground the LORD God formed every **beast of the field**, and every **fowl of the air**; and brought them unto Adam to see what he would call them: and whatsoever Adam called every living creature, that was the name thereof. And Adam gave names to all **cattle**, and to the **fowl of the air**, and to every **beast of the field**; but for Adam there was not found an help meet for him.

Does anyone notice something? God "formed" beasts and fowl here — but he brings before Adam beasts, fowl, and *cattle* — the domestic creatures! Where did they come from? The answer is that they were *already* in Eden (a special place set aside, because it was a garden), and that the "forming" of the beasts and fowl is an act of special creation, giving Adam samples of these beasts and fowls from outside Eden for the sake of presenting them to the earth's appointed king. (After all, why should a king have to wait for his subjects to wander in when he can have them brought to him at once?) In this passage the author clearly shows awareness of the cattle having already been created in G1, because he does **not** indicate their creation here, but assumes that they don't need to be created. Even without the pluperfect reading, G1 and G2 are fully consistent.

Read More!

<http://www.tektonics.org/jedp/creationtwo.html>

Chapter 8:

How Many "E's" in Elohim?

In the Old Testament in Hebrew, God is called *Elohim.* In Hebrew, a word ending –im is a plural, and so some people think that when God is called "Elohim" it refers to many gods – in other words, *polytheism.*

This is easily refuted by the point that although *Elohim* is a plural form, it is always paired with verbs in the *singular.* So what this word means is not many beings, but one being with many powers.

But there's another point to be made. The word *elohim* is sometimes used in the Old Testament of angels. What this tells us is that the word *elohim* doesn't have the same definition as our word *God.* Today we use "God" as a personal name of the being we worship. But the way *elohim* is used shows that it is a more general term, with a more abstract meaning, like the word "power" in the phrase, "electrical power."

In other words, *elohim* includes God, and also angels, but this does not mean the Bible teaches many gods (polytheism) as we use the word. It does teach that there is only one God worthy of worship, who created the world and everything in it, and in that sense, it already says that the God we worship is unique, and greater than any other god, real or imagined.

Read More!

<http://www.tektonics.org/lp/monoelohim.html>

Chapter 9:

The Big Fruit Scam

God leaves the Tree of Knowledge in the Garden of Eden. He tells Adam and Eve not to eat from it. They do. God jumps on them for it. *Wham!* The whole place is messed up.

Is this a case of "*entrapment*"? In other words, can we say that God set things up and so this wasn't fair?

Police are sometimes accused of using entrapment to catch criminals, and it can be used as a defense so that someone who is accused of a crime can go free.

A trip to the law library, though, tells us that Adam and Eve weren't victims of entrapment. Entrapment as a defense in court was first brought up in the case of *Sorrells vs. United States* in the late 1870s. Since then, a lot has been said about it, but it is fully agreed that "entrapment" only occurs when a police official intends to *encourage someone to commit a crime*, exercising direct influence on them. As that legal case says, "Entrapment is the conception and planning of an offense by an officer, and his procurement of its commission by one who would not have perpetrated it except for the trickery, persuasion, or fraud of the officer."

Let's explain by example.

1. A police officer who leaves a bale of marijuana in the street, and orders people who see him do it, "Don't touch it. Don't even mess with it," is *not* using entrapment.
2. A police officer who leaves a bale of marijuana in the street and says *nothing* to anyone about it, but instead waits around to see if anyone picks it up or smokes it, *may* be engaged in entrapment. This is where the courts have done a lot of talking, but entrapment is more likely to stick as a defense if the person who ends up committing the crime is not inclined to commit such crimes in the first place, or has no record of committing the crime, and yet the officer does something to actively

encourage the crime. (Such as asking, "Hey, wanna smoke some dope?" — repeated even after refusals.)

3. On the other hand, as the case says, "If the accused is found to be predisposed, the defense of entrapment may not prevail." So, "sting" operations (where an undercover police officer pretends to want to buy some drugs from a dealer) are not considered to be entrapment.

So which of these fits the Garden situation? The first one does, but do you know any police officer who would do things like *that*? Some might argue that the second is what actually happened in the Garden, but they would have a hard time justifying that, unless they could prove that God made the Tree of Knowledge impossible to resist, or Himself encouraged Adam and Eve to disobey His command, and we have no indication that that is the case. In fact, if anyone is guilty of entrapment in the story, it's the serpent!

Chapter 10:

Anachrophobia

An *anachronism* is a statement that doesn't make sense in the time the events recorded or reported happened. For example, if I told a story of a medieval knight living in 1200 AD, in which I said that he went home to watch a movie on his DVD player, that's an anachronism, because the DVD player hadn't been invented yet. (The TV had been invented, but no one watched because there was no place to plug it in.)

Some people say the Bible has anachronisms in it, but in some cases they are wrong. In other cases, what they're seeing is a change that was made by a later person who copied an older part of the Bible and found something that readers in his time would find hard to understand.

For example, back as early as the 1890s people used a phrase, "twenty three skidoo." It was something you said to someone when you wanted them to leave. Today we would say, "hit the road" or "get lost." Some of the claimed anachronisms in the Bible are places where later people who copied the Bible changed or added information to make it clear to readers in *their* time what was going on.

In the Bible, for example, 1 Chronicles 9:27 refers to a unit of money called a *daric*. The Chronicler describes King David as collecting ten thousand darics for the construction of the temple in Jerusalem. Critics say that the daric was named after king Darius of Persia, who lived over five hundred years after David. But this is not a mistake because the author of Chronicles was writing in a time when the daric was a known unit of money. The author was just "translating" for his readers who would not understand the worth of money in David's time – sort of like we might say people in France spend "millions of dollars" on wine and cheese even though France uses the euro as money.

The Bible isn't the only document we find this sort of thing in. We can also find "anachronisms" in non-Biblical texts, for the same reasons. For example, we can refer to the Romans crossing the "English Channel" even though in their time it was called the Litus Saxonicum.

We have to be careful when we say a text like the Bible has committed "anachronism." Most of the time, these were changes made in later copies to make sure that people always understood what the Bible was saying – sort of like the way some people don't like the King James Version because it says stuff like "thee" and "thou". When was the last time you heard someone talk like that outside of Thor in Marvel Comics?

Read More!

<http://www.tektonics.org/af/anachronisms.html>

Chapter 11:

To Be Seen, Or Not Be Seen

> John 1:18 No one has ever seen God, but God the One and Only, ho is at the Father's side, has made him known.
>
> Exodus 33:20 "But," he said, "you cannot see my face, for no one may see me and live."
>
> 1 Tim. 6:16 ...[God] alone is immortal and who lives in unapproachable light, whom no one has seen or can see.

There are many verses like these that say that God can't be seen. However, we know of many other verses where someone in the Bible says that they *see* God.

How do we answer this? There are different answers for each verse where someone says that they "see" God, but here are two broad answers that apply to all of them:

In the Old Testament, people can see "Yahweh" – it is "Elohim" that they cannot see. *Yahweh* and *Elohim* are two of many nouns (titles, names, etc.) used of God in the Old Testament. *Yahweh* is translated "the Lord" (all in capitals in some Bibles) while *Elohim* is translated "God." As we explained a few chapters back, the word *elohim* isn't exactly a proper name, but a descriptive noun like "deity" or "power". So it is sometimes used even of pagan gods. But you will find that only rarely does the Old Testament say *Elohim* was seen (Gen. 35:9, 2 Chr. 1:7), and since it is not really a proper name, it would mean that some display of God's power had been seen, not the person of God Himself.

However, even when people see *Yahweh* it is something which they express surprise at having seen and lived to tell about it (Genesis 32:30, Exodus 24:9-11). So even the passages that say Yahweh was "seen" show that there was an awareness that those who saw God would normally not be expected to survive.

What can't be seen is God Himself in His full glory. Exodus 33:20 makes this clear if you know what it is saying. "Face" was a metaphor for talking to or knowing a person directly – "face to face". God can be "seen" through incarnation as a human (John 14:7) but not directly, in His "natural" state. Put it this way: You can't stare at the sun, but you can look at the light it gives off and is reflected from it.

Read More!

<http://www.tektonics.org/uz/visiblegod.html>

Chapter 12:

JEDP

"JEDP" isn't the call letters of a radio station in Japan. It's a theory that the five books of Moses – Genesis, Exodus, Numbers, Leviticus, and Deuteronomy – were not written or authorized by Moses, but put together over hundreds of years by different guys in the history of the Jewish people. Those four guys are called J ("Jahwist," using J instead of Y to spell Yahweh, the name of God), E (for "Elohim"), D ("Deuteronomist") and P ("Priestly"). The idea is that D was one author, who just wrote Deuteronomy, while J and E wrote different parts of the rest at different times. Then P wove together all of the stuff by the other three to make the books of Moses.

In a place like this book, we can't offer a lot of details about JEDP because it would take too long. But we can give you a few pointers about it, and if you want to know more, then you can check the Read More entry at the end of this chapter.

First, JEDP depends a lot on assuming that Deuteronomy can be dated very late. JEDP usually argues that Deuteronomy is the "book of the law" found in the Temple during the time of King Hezekiah 2 Kings 22, and that it was actually written at that time by priests who pretended it was an older document. But there are a lot of good arguments against this. For example, Deuteronomy is in the format of an ancient treaty between a king (God) and his people (Israel), and it looks a lot more like the kind of treaties that were written when Moses would be alive (around 1400 BC) than the ones in the time of Hezekiah (around 700 BC). Maybe the strongest argument for JEDP here is that Deuteronomy mentions Moses' death at the very end, but this makes better sense as comment added by someone who copied the book for later people (see the chapter, "Anachrophobia"). It's not a good enough reason to date *the whole book* late because of one verse at the very end.

Second, JEDP theories don't account for ancient ways of writing. For example, a big deal is made of how three stories in Genesis (12:10-20, 20:1-18, and 26:1-11) seem basically the same. Critics don't understand why one author would write three stories the same way three times like this. But there was a good reason for one author to do this. Most people were illiterate in Bible times, and would have the story read or spoken aloud to them. Making the stories similar like this made them easier to remember.

This could easily be done without reporting history wrongly. (See the chapter, "Fictional Fiction.")

Third, JEDP theories rely a lot on how "divine names" are used. Back in the 1700s, the first person to suggest something like JEDP thought that it was very significant that some parts of the five books of Moses used the name "Yahweh" for God, while other parts used "Elohim." Since then the idea has been that these two names are used because they were written by different people (J and E) who preferred each name (and also different ideas about God). This argument has a number of serious problems.

For example, the J and E division isn't found all through the books of Moses. Some critics may make you think that the divine name division is clear throughout the five books, but in fact, it is only good through Genesis and a few of the first chapters of Exodus. After that, "Yahweh" is almost always used, although "Elohim" does make appearances. JEDP theorists say that the writers they call E and P stopped using "Elohim" so much after a certain point where Yahweh reveals Himself to Moses by the name Yahweh (Ex. 6:3), and this explains why the names no longer alternate the same way. But this explanation doesn't work because "Elohim" is still used a lot after Exodus 6:3. It also doesn't account for the fact that "Elohim" is not really a name (see the chapter, "How Many E's in Elohim?").

Also, we see the words "Yahweh" and "Elohim" used back and forth in later books of the Old Testament, but no one claims that they were written by J and E and then spliced together. Finally, pagan texts vary divine names of pagan gods the same way. For example, the god "Baal" was sometimes called "Hadad." Ancient gods collected names as a mark of honor!

Read More!

<http://www.tektonics.org/TK-J.html#jedp>

There are several articles at this location about the JEDP theory and specific claims made to support it.

Chapter 13:

Onan the Barbarian

> Gen. 38:9-10 But Onan knew that the offspring would not be his; so whenever he lay with his brother's wife, he spilled his semen on the ground to keep from producing offspring for his brother. What he did was wicked in the LORD's sight; so he put him to death also.

"Hey, that's not fair!"

Some people read this and think Onan didn't do anything wrong. As far as they can see, this is like God punishing someone for picking daisies.

But hold on a second. There are times when you think a man is just helping an old lady across the street, because you can't see the gun he has in his pocket which he's using to mug her once they both get to a less public place. To see the "gun" Onan is holding we need to know a little more about the kind of world these people lived in. Once we know about that, we find out that Onan did no less than *four* rotten, despicable things:

First: He refused to carry out his responsibility as the brother of the deceased. In this time of history, there was no such thing as Social Security or Medicaid. If you wanted to survive for a good long time, you needed help from your family – especially family that was younger than you. Meaning, children.

Onan's sister-in-law, Tamar – his brother's wife – was in serious trouble. Her husband had died, and they had no children, so when she got older, she'd have no one to help her survive. The people who lived in this time had a solution to the problem of younger widows like this one: The nearest male relative to the deceased husband would help the widow get pregnant. That way she could have a child, and have their own version of "social security." This is what is called *levirate marriage* (Deuteronomy 25). Ruth and Boaz were an example of this type of marriage.

The important thing to remember is that in doing what he did Onan was saying to his brother's wife, "I don't care if you die early because you have no one to help you."

Second: Onan not only refused, but *repeatedly* refused. If you read the verse in Hebrew, you find out that the meaning is that *whenever* Onan lay with Tamar — not just once, but *every time* – he would refuse to fulfill his duties, and spill his seed on the ground. Onan was a "repeat offender" and had plenty of chances to fulfill his obligation.

Third, Onan not only repeatedly refused, but *pretended* that he wasn't refusing. If Onan was not willing to do his part, all he had to do was say so. It would have been an insult, and he would have had to suffer disgrace (see Numbers 27:8-11 for an example of what would happen) for being such a jerk and not helping out a helpless widow, but it was still his option. Instead, he decided to go for having his cake and eating it too, by having the pleasure of being with Tamar, while avoiding the obligation. How selfish can you get!?

Finally, Onan was setting it up so that *he* would get the big bucks and leave Tamar penniless and helpless. If Tamar had no heir born to her, guess who got the family's inheritance? I'll give you a hint: His name started with "O"!

So here's the scoop: Don't feel sorry for "Onan the Barbarian." He was trying to condemn Tamar to a slow death while at the same time living it up at her expense.

Chapter 14:

Bad News for the Firstborn

Isaac. Jephthah's daughter. Jesus. What do these three people have in common?

Answer: All three are examples of people who are the subject of argument often made: *Why does God allow human sacrifice?* In fact, isn't human sacrifice forbidden in the Bible?

Let's answer the second question first, and the answer may surprise you. The answer is *no* – the Bible does not forbid human sacrifice, exactly. What it does forbid is sacrifice of ***children*** – check the many passages on the subject (like Leviticus 18:21) and you will find that it is *children* who are mentioned. And the specific reason given why it is wrong is because it is murder – the victim of the sacrifice is innocent and unwilling.

Now this being the case, one of the three examples given, Jesus, is already off the list, because he was not a child when he died. (Isaac and Jephthah's daughter may not have been either, but we'll look closer at them anyway.) But, you may ask, isn't it still immoral to have human sacrifice – even if, as in the clear case of Jesus, it was a willing adult?

We believe Jesus died in our place. Now if you think this is immoral, then it is also immoral to push someone out of the way of a car, so that you are hit instead? Is it immoral to take a bullet for someone to keep them from being killed? Most people think that this sort of thing is heroic, not immoral. As a matter of fact, ancient people especially had no problem with the idea of someone dying in the place of another. (We'll talk more about this in the chapter on Jesus dying for our sins.)

But then what about Isaac, and Jephthah's daughter?

In the case of Isaac, we have someone who may or may not have been an adult (estimates of his age range from 15 to 37). We aren't told enough to say. However, it is likely that Abraham knew that Isaac would not actually end up dead: God had promised him that Isaac would be the son through which he would beget many descendants. In fact, Abraham tells his servants that both he and Isaac will return, so it is very clear that he either did not expect an actual sacrifice to occur, or else expected that Isaac would be raised from the dead. It is also likely that Isaac was a willing sacrifice, because he was strong enough to carry a load of wood (Genesis 22:6) up a mountainside and could certainly have resisted his elderly father.

Either way, since Isaac was never actually killed, this cannot be taken as a true example of human sacrifice.

Then what about the example of Jephthah's daughter in Judges 11? Here the evidence shows that there was no sacrifice. First of all, Jephthah says he will give God a "burnt offering" as a way of thanking God for his success, but burnt offerings had to do with judgment, not with giving thanks. Because of this, Jephthah probably meant "burnt offering" in the sense of something he will permanently give up. Second, Jephthah's vow to make an offering would have been public and known to his entire village, including his daughter, so this would mean she heard what he said in his pledge, then later came out of the house first *on purpose*, which makes little sense if she knew she was going to be killed. (It may be that she did this because she wanted to be dedicated to God's service.) Finally, when his daughter goes out to the wilderness with friends to mourn, she does not say that she is mourning being killed; she is mourning because she will always be a virgin (never married), which would also describe a woman in service to God.

So when you get down to it, you can't even find any real "human sacrifice" in the Bible in the first place.

Read More!

<http://www.tektonics.org/gk/jepthah.html>
<http://www.christian-thinktank.com/sacra.html>
<http://www.christian-thinktank.com/qkilisak.html>

Chapter 15:

Wishy-Washy Deity?

For this one, I have to use King James' version... please don't fall asleep!

> Malachi 3:6 "For I am the LORD; I change not."

> Numbers 23:19 "God is not a man, that he should lie; neither the son of man, that he should repent..."

These verses indicate that God isn't the sort to flip sides. But what, it is asked, of these verses?

> Genesis 6:6,7 "And it repented the Lord that he had made man on the earth . . . And the Lord said, I will destroy man whom I have created from the face of the earth . . . for it repenteth me that I have made him."

> Jonah 3:10 ". . . and God repented of the evil, that he had said that he would do unto them; and he did it not."

So what is the answer?

The ability to be *omniscient*, to know all things, must be understood. God is timeless. Past, present and future for God can be seen as a whole. God also knows how things would turn out if *differently* had a different path been taken at every potential choice-making nexus. God knew you would turn left at Starbucks this morning, but He also knows what *would have* happened had you turned right.

A prophet wasn't just someone who was a teller of the future. Prophets were also messengers and encouragers who gave God's message to people so that they could change and God would forgive them. Jeremiah 18:7-10 says:

> If at any time I announce that a nation or kingdom is to be uprooted, torn down and destroyed, and if that nation I warned repents of its evil, then I will relent and not inflict on it the disaster I had planned. And if at another time I announce that a nation or kingdom is to be built up and planted, and if it does evil in my sight and does not obey me, then I will reconsider the good I had intended to do for it.

So it's pointless to complain like Jonah did, when, for example, God didn't act in judgment on

Nineveh (Jonah 3:10). We may read it as a definitive prophecy, no exceptions possible, but it would be understood by the hearers as allowing for the disaster to be avoided if they followed God's instructions.

But then, what about those places where it says God "repents," despite places that say He never does? What we need to remember is that the same word can often have a range of meanings, especially in a language like Hebrew which had way fewer words than English. (Remember, they had only a few thousand words; we have more than a million!) It's clear from the use of the word in Genesis 6 and Jonah 3 that it is used to simply mean having regrets over a specific action (Genesis 6) that was *not* immoral, but had regrettable consequences (such as, we give a new car as a gift, which is good, but the person wrecks it, which is bad), or not performing a threatened action (Jonah 3), which Jeremiah already says God can do. In Numbers 23:19 the word is used of going back on a pledge (which would be immoral), and Ezekiel 24 is simply saying that it is too late for people to turn back because God has given them enough chances.

Read More!

<http://www.tektonics.org/gk/godchangemind.html>

Chapter 16:

Reading Leviticus Can Be Fun!

Do you ever read laws in the Old Testament and think to yourself, "What was *that* for?"

There's a funny book I read once that listed strange laws…in America. It included things like a law in a small town that didn't allow people to bring lions into movie theaters. A law like that may seem silly, and maybe it is, but chances are it was made because someone once brought a lion into a movie theater and then argued that he could because there was no law against it!

If laws in the Bible seem strange, it may be because of the different ways people did things in Bible times. For example, Deut. 22:8 requires you to build your roof with a border around it. It may make no sense until you realize that people in ancient Israel (and even in modern nations in the Near East today) live, work, and sleep on their roof like it was a regular room of the house. So this was a very important law for safety.

But many of the laws that seem silly to us have to do with a concept called *ritual purity*. For example, in Leviticus 13, a man with just a spot of leprosy is called "unclean," but a man who is covered with leprosy all over his body is called "clean." How is it that this man is declared "clean" while being covered *all over* with leprosy? The answer is that "clean" refers to *ceremonial* cleanness - not physical cleanness. He is entirely covered with leprosy, so you might say he is "all one color" – he's uniform, the same all over. That's good for a case of *ceremonial* cleanness. This is also why there were laws against things like wearing a garment made of two types of cloth (Lev. 19:19).

Ceremonial cleanness, or ritual purity, was very important to ancient people because the world they lived in was an unsafe and dangerous place. Ritual purity gave them a reassurance and a comfort, sort of like a habit we might have ourselves that makes us feel better – like not stepping on spit on the sidewalk, or pushing our vegetables all to one side of the plate before eating them.

For many people in the world, however – including the Hebrews – ritual purity was and is much more important than that, because being ritually pure also meant you were imitating God.

But what about the law today – does it serve any purpose? Jesus said:

> Matthew 5:18 For verily I say unto you, Till heaven and earth pass, one jot or one tittle shall in no wise pass from the law, till all be fulfilled.(cf. Luke 16:17)

"If this is true," some people have asked, "why are you violating the law by eating pork and wearing polyester suits? Those would be forbidden by the Old Testament law. Christians just pick and choose what they want to follow."

There's a valid question here: What is the role of the Law in the life of the Christian today? Do we need to trash our polyester? If we are true believers, do we need to execute witches? And finally, is the covenant still "good" with Israel today?

To answer these questions we need to start with some understanding about what is in the Old Testament law.

First, some laws are universal moral laws. This includes *do not steal*, *do not kill*, and others. There is no disagreement that these laws should indeed be continued to be obeyed today, so we don't need to discuss them further.

Second, some laws are *cultural universals.* By this I mean laws geared to Israel's culture, that have a universal moral law behind them. Deut. 22:8, which I mentioned before, would be an example of this. Another would be the law against trimming your beard (Lev. 19:27). Many scholars think this law relates to pagan practices that cut facial hair for magical purposes. So the universal behind this cultural would be, don't do the occult.

Finally, there are ceremonial laws. Instructions for building the Ark of the Covenant, for example, are definitely in this, as are sacrificial laws. What else belongs in here? Most likely the dietary laws belong here, because their purpose was to make the Jews "stand out" and to serve as a testimony to their difference in the most intimate ancient setting, that of meal fellowship.

With that in mind, what does Jesus mean when he says he came to "fulfill" the law? To *fulfill* God's law was to confirm it by obedience; whereas to *destroy* (some versions say *annul*) the law was to treat it as if it was no longer valid. Jesus is answering claims that he was breaking the law by affirming that he didn't. (See more in the chapter titled, "Jesus the Hypocrite.") Yet he also says that nothing will pass from the law until all is fulfilled, so doesn't this mean the law is still around and needs to be obeyed?

There's a simple way to answer this. We can argue that "all was fulfilled" when Jesus rose from the dead.

This would make sense because it was at about this time, at the Last Supper, when Jesus offered a new covenant, which means a person could opt out of the old one. The book of Hebrews also says that the old covenant is passing away (8:13) at that time, so it seems clear that the new replaced the old.

The covenant of law itself is past. So what good is the law to us, and how can we still use it as an example for some moral issues? Deuteronomy, which is where the Old Testament law was put into writing, is an example of a contract. Now if you want to rent an apartment, you can get an idea what the landlord likes if you read a lease that someone signed before you came. It will have rules in it that will give you an idea what the landlord thinks is wrong or immoral. Even though we have a new covenant (lease), the old one can still give us an idea what the landlord's priorities are, and what rules he might want us to follow. This is why we can still point to laws against homosexuality to say that the Bible teaches against it, but also why we don't execute witches as the law says to. We didn't sign the contract that is Deuteronomy, so we don't have to enforce the penalties, but Deuteronomy still tells us about things God doesn't approve of.

So what can we learn from the law, based on those three categories? All of the ceremonial laws have been superseded by Christ. (Hebrews is the New Testament book that lays this out the best, though see Matt. 26:28.) They pointed towards Christ and the unified body of believers. Because of this, also, there is no need for the laws of diet and not wearing two types of fabric woven together. These things were commanded to make the people of God unique, and stand out in their world, as a certain people reserved to God. The new covenant is open to all who come in, so it would be inappropriate to enforce laws that made people separate.

All we have left are the moral laws that apply at all times, and there are many discussions as to which laws qualify as that sort of thing. The law remains something we can learn a lot from, even if we're not obliged to obey every bit of it.

Read More!

<http://www.tektonics.org/af/cleanman.html>
<http://www.tektonics.org/lp/lawrole.html>
<http://www.christian-thinktank.com/finaltorah.html>

Chapter 17:

Daddy Pays Up

Deut. 24:16 says, "Fathers shall not be put to death for their children, nor children put to death for their fathers; each is to die for his own sin." But Deut. 5:9 says, "You shall not bow down to them or worship them; for I, the LORD your God, am a jealous God, punishing the children for the sin of the fathers to the third and fourth generation of those who hate me..." How can both of these be true? One says that each person pays for their own sin, while the other says that someone can be punished for the sin of another person, a relative.

We need to understand why Deut. 24:16 was written. It refers to something called *vicarious punishment* that was found in the laws of other nations at the time of Moses. This type of punishment allowed the ruler of a nation to kill someone's child for a crime committed by a parent. Deut. 24:16 is specifically written against this practice.

Deut. 5:9 is about a different subject. When it and similar verses speak of punishment of third and fourth generations, these have to do with specific crimes against the majesty of God, such as Achan's sin (Josh. 7). These crimes were much more serious, and it is assumed that the whole household was part of the crime – either by helping with it, or covering it up. (Keep in mind that families lived together in big groups, so that "three or four generations" usually were alive at the same time in the same house. You couldn't do a lot of stuff by yourself in secret – see what we said in the chapter called "Culture Shock" about privacy.)

Read More!

<http://www.tektonics.org/lp/paydaddy.html>

Chapter 18:

Something Rotten 'bout Akhenaten

Critics look in all kinds of places for parallels to Biblical beliefs, because they often hope they can find something similar which they can say the

Jewish or Christian religions "stole" an idea from (as opposed to being something God revealed, or was otherwise true). Here's one of my favorites from the Old Testament: The idea that *monotheism*, the belief in one god, is not a Hebrew original, but was borrowed from the Egyptian Pharaoh Akhenaten.

Let's start by listing, in full, the similarities between Atenism (as we'll call Akhenaten's religion) and Jewish monotheism. They are:

1. Both believe in one God who is a Creator and sustainer of the universe.

That's it.

Now if this is all there is to the similarities, you got to wonder what side of the bed some people got up on this morning (or fell off of). Coming up with an idea that there's only one God (rather than several or none) is sort of like coming up with an idea to put salt on your dinner. It's just something we'd expect people to think of even without help.

More than this, there are a lot of differences between Atenism and Judaism. We all know how many rules God handed down in the Pentateuch. Atenism had no rules or laws (not even against taking a lion into a movie theater). Aten was the creator (though we know of no "creation story"), but he didn't hand out any special favors, or heal the sick, or forgive the sinner. He didn't have any ceremonies, like God did in the Old Testament, other than a basic daily sacrifice.

In addition, Akhenaten regarded himself as the actual child of Aten, and if you wanted something, you had to go to Akhenaten first and talk to him. (Make an appointment.) Moses was a sort of go-between himself, between God and Israel, but the everyday Israelite could pray right to God if they wanted to.

The fact is, there is little that is the same about Atenism and Judaism, and scholars of Egyptian religion will say the same thing.

Read More!

<http://www.tektonics.org/copycat/akhenaten.html>

Chapter 19:

Can You Dig It?

"Archaeology proves the Bible."
"Archaeology disproves the Bible."

Google these two phrases sometime and see what happens. You'll find plenty of websites that say one or the other. Which one is right?

Actually, neither one is even said the right way. "The Bible" is too broad a category – we should only refer to *specific events* recorded in the Bible. And "prove" (or "disprove") is too strong a word. Better words to use would be "confirmed" or even "corroborated." So using those words, which is true – has archaeology confirmed (or not confirmed) events in the Bible?

We sure won't be able to answer all the possible questions here, but we can make a few points.

First, many conclusions in archaeology are still being debated. Archaeology involves a lot of work, and a lot of time. Arguments change over time as more stuff is dug up. The best known example may be the city of Jericho. There's still plenty of debate over how much of the Bible's story of Joshua's conquest has been supported by archaeological finds (or some say, not supported).

Second, lack of evidence does not automatically disconfirm something in the Bible. For example, a lot of critics say that there's no archaeological evidence for the Exodus in the wilderness. They think that if that many people were running around in the desert, they should have left all kinds of evidence behind. But that's not true. For one thing, ancient people lived in a world where resources were scarce. It was not likely they ever threw anything away on purpose. (For example, when Native Americans hunted the buffalo, they used *all* of it – even its excrement, which they used for fuel.) Also, natural conditions such as wind and rain can wipe out evidence. For comparison, there were a people called the Scythians who lived on the plains in what is now Russia. They were nomads like the Israelites, and lived there for hundreds of years – but we have no evidence left from them except for stuff from their kings (tombs and jewelry). In fact, we don't even know how they did some things, like bathe themselves. (Maybe they didn't!)

Third, some scholars read too much into what the Bible says, and then reach wrong conclusions based on archaeology. For example, one archaeologist says, "Despite Judah's prominence in the Bible... there is no archaeological indication until the eighth century BCE that this small and rather isolated highland area...possessed any particular importance." But where does the Bible ever say that Judah was anything *but* "small and isolated"? Where does it say Judah was "important" in any way that archaeology would be concerned with? This is like saying, "Despite how often Joe mentioned himself in his biography, there is no indication on his block that he was anyone particularly important."

The archaeologist has confused the Bible's concern with Judah with a claim that it was somehow considered important in ways that archaeologists would look at (such as, having big cities or a lot of wealth).

We'll talk about one example of Bible archaeology later, when we come to the chapter on Nazareth, where Jesus lived.

Read More!

<http://www.christian-thinktank.com/noai.html>
<http://www.tektonics.org/af/exoduslogistics.html>

Chapter 20:

You Have An Image Problem

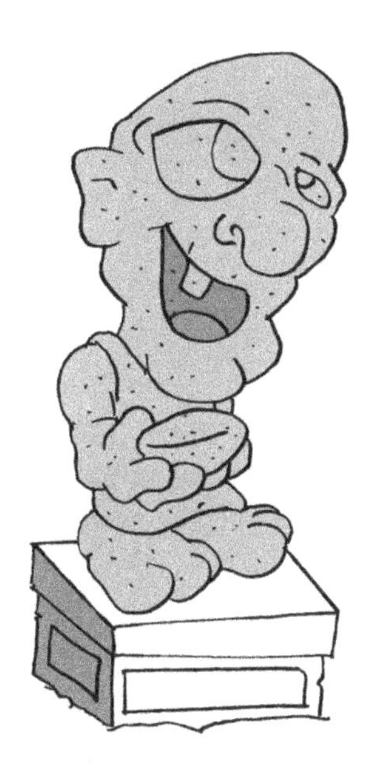

Hey, I'm sorry…modern versions of the Bible (the more cool ones) don't make this as clear, so I need to use King James again!

> Exodus 20:4 "Thou shalt not make unto thee any graven image, or any likeness of anything

> that is in heaven . . . earth . . . water." (See also Lev. 26:1, Deut. 27:15)

This commandment is one of the Big Ten. It must have been a pretty important one. But you might just ask yourself, what about this sort of thing, then?

> Exodus 25:18 "And thou shalt make two cherubims of gold, of beaten work shalt thou make them."

> I Kings 7:15,16,23,25 "For he [Solomon] cast two pillars of brass . . . and two chapiters of molten brass . . . And he made a molten sea . . . it stood upon twelve oxen . . . [and so on]"

Wait a minute. Weren't these things "graven images"? What about paintings? What about your Britney Spears poster? What about other kinds of art, like even the cartoon at the top of this chapter? (I think that's Goofus, the Babylonian god of stupidity, by the way.) *Would God come down on us from Sinai for drawing stuff like this?* **Whoa**.

The answer is that **no**, these are not graven images. The word "image" (and "likeness", which is a synonym) doesn't mean just any kind of statue or picture.

People who lived in Bible times believed that by carving an idol (an image) you could give your god a place to come down and talk to you. You might say that it was a sort of telephone booth to the gods.

(I guess the pagans used to make calls using the "Southern Baal" telephone company.)

God didn't want Israel making images because it would imply that God was just like the pagan gods – you could just whistle (or sacrifice a goat, maybe) and He'd be there. God said that prophets were His instrument for talking to people – images were out.

God also didn't want the people setting up images to pagan gods because by making these images, it implied that these other gods were real and you could talk to them.

What this means is that the cherubim on the Ark of the Covenant, the oxen, modern works of art – are all not forbidden by the commandment, because no one made them so that a god could come speak to them. Same goes for paintings and yes, cartoons like that one of Goofus.

If you hear one of my cartoons talking – see a doctor.

Chapter 21:

I Didn't See a Miracle!

The Bible records several spectacular miracles. This raises a good question: If these impressive events actually took place, why don't we have records of them outside the Bible? Shouldn't there be a lot of documents that mention them?

The answer to this question is **no**, and there are a couple of good reasons for this. Let's use the parting of the Rea Sea in Exodus as an example.

The first and most important is that the number of people who actually could *write* a document mentioning some Biblical miracle was very small. In the time of Jesus, no more than ten percent of all the people in the Roman Empire were even literate. In the time of Moses, when the Red Sea was parted, the number would have been even lower, maybe less than one percent. We can hardly expect more documents if there's so few people to write them in the first place. And then of course, that document has to survive thousands of years into our own day, which is a tall order: We know that we have very little of the original literature of the ancient world.

The second reason is that the only people who would usually be interested in making such a document, would be people who thought the miracle was a *good* thing. That means the Bible itself is the document we'd expect to hear about these miracles from. Egypt's kings would have no interest in recording the miracle of the Red Sea parting – it would be something that made them look bad. We know that their Pharaohs often did not report their losses, or else put a "spin" on them to make themselves look better. We also know that they tried to erase things that were considered embarrassing. (For example, Akhenaten – the guy we mentioned a few chapters ago – was considered such an embarrassment to later Egyptian pharaohs that they tried to destroy all his monuments and pretend that he never existed.)

In light of all this, it isn't surprising that the Bible is the only record we have of even the most spectacular miracles it records. And this isn't surprising either when we make a comparison to how well-recorded spectacular *natural* events were. For example, in 79 AD, Mount Vesuvius erupted and buried the city of Pompeii, in Italy. This was a spectacular event that killed as many as 60,000 people and would have had effects (smoke, earthquakes) that would have been seen as far away as Rome, where millions of people lived. But all we have in literature left to us mentioning it is *one* record by Pliny the Younger, who only included the story because his uncle was killed in the eruption and a friend of his asked him to tell him about it.

Read More!

<http://www.christian-thinktank.com/5felled.html>

Chapter 22:

Totally Outrageous

Here's something I'll bet you'll run into a lot:

1. A person finds some event in the Biblical text that they find offensive: The slaughter of the Canaanites; the stoning of the man who picked up sticks on the Sabbath, and so on.
2. They talk about this event in such a way as to say, that by itself, the event is enough of a moral outrage that there can be no argument or counter to it.

This isn't really an argument, of course. It's just a substitute for real argument, one that uses emotion to persuade rather than reason. I like to call it "argument by outrage."

But we don't convict people of murder by going on about how horrible murder is. We look at the evidence and decide whether they are guilty. In some cases we may find that a person killed someone else for a valid reason (in war, self-defense, and so on). Take these two statements:

- Hitler exterminated 6 million Jews.
- Blethkorp exterminated 6 million Refrons.

We are right to be upset at the first one. But why? The obvious reason is that we know about Hitler and we know from the evidence that he was morally wrong.

"Argument by outrage" makes statements like the second and simply assumes that it is as bad as the first. But what if we start fleshing out the second one, so that:

1. "Blekthorp" is the leader of the Harlanian race, a peaceful people who only wish to be left alone.
2. The "Refrons" are a predatory and parasitical race — say like *Star Trek's* Borg — whose only goal is to assimilate others into their culture or destroy those they consider inferior.

Now that we have the context, how can someone make an "argument by outrage"? (Sure, this is an extreme example, but the point is still the same.) We would hope that anyone would agree that the Harlanians have a right to defend themselves. If the Refrons refuse to give up and are willing to fight to the last to achieve their goal, is it a moral outrage that the Harlanians exterminated 6 million of them? What if the total population of Refrons was somewhere around 70 *billion* and killing 6 million was the only way to get the Refrons to decide that the cost of conquest was too high? (Actually, this is the sort of argument that people made when it was decided whether or not to drop a nuclear bomb on Japan back in the 1940s.)

Before anyone can put forward an "argument by outrage" as more than just talk, there's a lot they need to prove. Let's take as an example the Canaanites in the Bible. God ordered Israel to drive out and if necessary make war against and kill these people. It's not enough to just say this and assume it is unfair. We need to show:

1) **That the Canaanites didn't have a chance to change their ways**. In this case, the Canaanites saw and knew of what happened in Egypt. This is why one of their groups, the Gibeonites, used deceit to forge a treaty with Israel. They knew what was coming if they didn't. They had plenty of time to change their ways.
2) **That the Canaanites were not bad.** But this won't be easy to do. Archaeological evidence shows that the Canaanites themselves violently destroyed other people to take their land from them. Different kinds of evidence also show that they practiced violent and immoral religious rites, including child sacrifice.

In other words, what needs to be shown is that something like the war against the Canaanites was not the equivalent to a justly-deserved sentence. It can't just be assumed that it was bad because people were killed.

Read More!

<http://www.tektonics.org/lp/outrage.html>
<http://www.christian-thinktank.com/rbutcher1.html>
<http://www.christian-thinktank.com/qamorite.html>
<http://www.christian-thinktank.com/midian.html>

Chapter 23:

The Bible's Wild Kingdom

The Bible never mentions cats. Did you know that? It does mention other animals, though, and there are times when critics think it is wrong about them. Let's look at some examples.

#1: Cud Chewers

> Lev. 11:6 The rabbit, though it chews the cud, does not have a split hoof; it is unclean for you.

This is one of the most popular objections in the skeptical book, and it's basically this: *Rabbits are not ruminants; they practice refection.* Refection is a process in which rabbits eat their own dung mixed with undigested material. The Hebrew does not use the word for "dung". Therefore this passage is wrong.

Two issues come up: the definition of "cud" and that of "chewing." Let's take a close look at the Hebrew version of both.

The word for "cud" is *gerah*, and it is used nowhere in the Old Testament besides this verse in Leviticus and a parallel verse in Deuteronomy. We have only this context to help us decide what it means in terms of the Mosaic law.

Second, refection is a process whereby rabbits pass pellets of partially digested food, which they chew on (along with the waste material) in order to give their stomachs another go at getting the nutrients out. It is not just "dung" that the rabbits are eating, which is probably why the Hebrew word for "dung" was not used here.

Compare this with what cows and some other animals do, rumination, which is what we call "chewing the cud." They regurgiate (throw up!) partially digested food in little clumps called cuds, and chew it a little more while mixing it with saliva. (Don't try this at your student union building.)

Partially digested food is a common element here. So the Hebrew word simply refers to any *partially digested food.*

Our other key word here is *'alah,* which translates as "chews" in the quote above but really means "bring up." This word is found in some form on literally every page of the Old Testament. This is because it is a word that encompasses many concepts other than "bring up." It also refers to Israel being brought out of Egypt (Josh. 24:17), Samuel offering a sacrifice (1 Sam. 7:10), and warriors lifting swords (Nahum 3:3).

What this means is that *'alah* isn't specific to regurgitation or any other process. It refers to any kind of motion. The rabbit is an animal that does make his previously digested material to "come" out of the body (though in a different way than a ruminant does) and does thereafter does chew "predigested material." The mistake is in our applying of the scientific terms of rumination to something that does not require it.

#2: Four Feet Good, Six Feet Bad

Here's another where I have to use King James to explain it for me:

> Lev. 11:20-3 All fowls that creep, going upon all four, shall be an abomination unto you. Yet these may ye eat of every flying creeping thing that goeth upon all **four**, which have

> legs above their feet, to leap withal upon the earth; even these of them ye may eat; the locust after his kind, and the bald locust after his kind, and the beetle after his kind, and the grasshopper after his kind. But all other flying creeping things, **which have four feet**, shall be an abomination unto you.

Is this an error — since insects have six feet, not four, and since "fowl" have two feet, not four? The reference to "fowl" is thought by some skeptics to refer to birds, but the word used here is *'owph*, which means a creature with wings — it is the same word used in verse 21 (flying). The reference in both cases is to insects. Now we might be cute here and call this a poetic phrase (like, "crawling around on all fours"), and this is partially right. But there is an even better - and more correct - answer.

The big back legs on the locust, etc. were not counted as "legs" in the same sense as the other legs. Let's use an illustration from a book you probably read in school (or saw the movie) — George Orwell's *Animal Farm.* In that story, Snowball the pig invented the slogan, "four legs good, two legs bad" to exclude humans from Animal Farm society. The geese and other birds objected, because they had only two legs. Snowball explained (more clearly in the book than in the movie) that in animal terms, the birds' wings counted as legs because they were limbs of propulsion (or motion), not manipulation (moving things), as a human's arms and hands were.

Now notice the difference in Leviticus above — referring to "legs above the feet" for leaping. The "feet" are different from the "legs above the feet" because of their difference in function. They are legs, but in a different sense than the "four" legs which are just called "feet." We are being told of two types of legs: The "on all four" legs (which are *nowhere* called legs; they are only called "feet" [v. 23]), and the "leaping legs." It is clear that the Hebrews regarded the two large, hopping hind limbs of the locust and the other insects of the same type, which are the only types of insects mentioned here (we now translate "beetle" as "cricket"), as something different than the other four limbs - perhaps because they were used primarily for vertical propulsion, whereas the other limbs were for scurrying around.

Unacceptable? The alternative is to say that the Hebrews - who ate these things **raw**, for crying out loud - didn't see that these bugs had six legs. Maybe they closed their eyes before putting them in their mouths...?

#3: Not a Bug's Life

> Proverbs 6:6-7 Go to the ant, you sluggard; consider its ways and be wise! It has no commander, no overseer or ruler…

There are some critics who say that this verse is wrong because ants do have a "queen." But that is no more than a case of us imposing human terms by analogy (what is called *anthropomorphizing*). The queen ant is mostly just an egg factory the ants care for. She doesn't make decisions like sending embassies to other anthills (unless in response to an attack, which is also something instinctual). The ants don't rule each other, or make decisions; it's all instinct, which is sort of the point of Proverbs 6:6. It seems that some critics have been watching *Antz* or *A Bug's Life* and been thinking that they are documentaries!

#4: Bat Bird!

> Lev. 11:13, 19 These are the birds you are to detest and not eat because they are detestable...And the stork, the heron after her kind, and the lapwing, and the bat.

Is there a biological blunder here? After all, bats aren't birds; they're mammals.

No, this is not a mistake, except in English translation. The scientific definition of what a "bird" was did not exist in the time of Moses (and wouldn't exist for thousands of years). Classification of animals and things was by function or form when Moses wrote. In this case, the word we translate "fowls" means simply "owner of a wing". And a bat does own wings.

Read More!

<http://www.tektonics.org/af/cudchewers.html>
<http://www.tektonics.org/af/buglegs.html>
<http://www.tektonics.org/lp/ostrich.html>
<http://www.tektonics.org/af/ants.html>
<http://www.tektonics.org/af/batbird.html>

Chapter 24:

Elisha and the Two Bears

2 Kings 2:23-24 From there Elisha went up to Bethel. As he was walking along the road, some youths came out of the town and jeered at him. “Go on up, you baldhead!” they said. “Go on up, you baldhead!” He turned around, looked at them and called down a curse on them in the name of the LORD. Then two bears came out of the woods and mauled forty-two of the youths.

So what's up with this, huh?

If you believe certain people out there who've looked into the background of the Bible as deeply as, say, they've looked into subatomic physics, then what we have here is a case of some crusty old prophet getting his shorts in a wad just because 42 little kids called him "bald". In fact, his shorts got so wadded that he called out two wild bears to kill every single one of them. Now **that's** one mean old guy. He probably called the SWAT team any time some kid touched a blade of grass on his lawn, too.

When you start to think about this story, though, and check things out, it's not that simple. Let's do that by asking some questions.

Little kids? He's killing little kids??

No, he's not. King James may have been a nice guy sometimes, but he didn't always get the language right. Certain people may want you to think that Elisha put this move on kids barely old enough to stop watching *Sesame Street*. That's flat out wrong. The Hebrew word used here (*yaled*) is used in other places in the Bible of boys between **twelve and thirty years old**. One of those words described Isaac (Genesis 22:12) when he was in his early twenties, and Joseph (Genesis 37:2) when he was seventeen years old. It described army men in 1 Kings 20:14-15.

However old these kids were, though, they were old enough to recognize a prophet of God and insult him - which means whatever the *physical* age of these "children" was, their brain functions were advanced enough so that they should have known better and should be held responsible for what they did.

As an aside, it's also wrong to picture Elisha as a crusty old man. He went on to live 60 more years, so he must have been about the same age as these kids. (You may say, "Yeah, but he was bald so he had to be old." We'll get to that in a minute.)

Hey, but come on. He's KILLING these kids.

No, that's not true either. The word used for what was done to them ("tare") means to break, rip or open. It's used for things like chopping a piece of wood or the splitting of the Red Sea. There's nothing that says anyone was killed here, unless you believe that bears split people in half.

In fact, because of the way the word is used elsewhere in the Bible, and because of the way bears are known to attack people, there are only two real possibilities:

1) It means that the bears scratched them with their claws or used their teeth. The word used could mean as little as a single scratch that breaks the skin. And here's something to think about: Two bears. At least 42 kids. Okay, how did just **two** bears manage that? Did they go after just two, and meanwhile the other 40 or more just stood there waiting in line for their turn? What this tells us is that these kids didn't do the smart thing and either run, or even just try to help the first people attacked get away. There's no way **42** of them got scratched up unless they *decided to go on the offensive against the bears*. That sounds

like a bad case of overconfidence – and like if it hadn't been there, there'd have been a lot less than 42 people given some sort of scratch.

If you think this seems far-fetched, you may also want to keep in mind that the bears were most likely Syrian brown bears. They're extinct in Palestine now, but they are very small (about 400 pounds!), and bears are timid by nature in the first place. In the 20th century, only 45 people were killed by bears in Canada and Alaska combined. To say that 42 people were killed by two bears in this single episode – and very small bears, at that – takes a lot of straining.

2) It means that the gang itself was "divided," with no sort of harm done (though it may have been). In 2 Samuel 23:16 the same word is used to describe how some men "broke through" an enemy army. So what this may mean is that the gang members all "split" – ran off in different directions.

But all they did was make fun of his bald head!

Not so. There are a lot more serious matters going on here. Look at the context. It says 42 were hurt, but what's a group of 42 kids doing banded together like this? In fact, if only 42 were hurt, how many were actually *in* the crowd in the first place? Fifty? A hundred?

But even if there were just 42 and the bears managed to bat a thousand, you have to ask yourself what so many of them were doing together. If you walked outside and there were **forty-two** people gathered on the sidewalk calling you any sort of name together, are you going to think there's nothing else bad going to happen?

Being called "baldy" wasn't all that was up here. If Elisha was a young man, and he really was bald at this time, he may have shaved his head on purpose as a sign of mourning Elijah, who had just ascended into heaven (notice how they also said, "go on up" – maybe talking about that ascension). In that case, they may have been making fun of his mourning, so it would be like barging into a funeral and making fun of someone crying over a person who just died that they cared about. Whatever the reason, it's a sure bet that they had more in mind than name-calling.

In fact, think of this: Life was very hard back then. Today we'd ask, "Why weren't these kids in school?" Back then we'd ask, "Why aren't these kids home helping their family plant and harvest crops, watching flocks, or doing what else was needed to survive day by day?" Some scholars have compared this to a modern street gang, and that's not far off from the truth. No, they wouldn't be stealing the hubcaps off of chariots or anything like that, but let's try things like robbery and banditry (remember the Good Samaritan story?) and maybe theft of animals from farmsteads. That's no prank in that day and age, but a really serious offense that could lead to the starvation of a family of innocents.

Back then, every family member was required to make a contribution in order to help the family survive - because there were no social services, no welfare checks, no supermarkets to stock up from in case your pantry was raided. So we have to ask again: Why were these kids banded together in such large numbers, and then, why were they not at home contributing to the survival of their own families? That they were banded together in such large numbers tells us that they were indeed a back-then version of a street gang —rovers who survived on their own, probably by robbing others of their lives and property; or else hoodlums banded together for the specific purpose of harming Elisha.

If you had 42 or more people coming down on you, I'll bet *you* wouldn't mind some help from a couple of bears.

(By the way, the people of Israel had been warned by God in Leviticus 26:21-22 that God would "send wild animals" against them if they didn't listen to Him. So they were warned that things like this could happen.)

So let's sum up what actually happened here. Elisha was walking along just minding his own business. This motivated group of *at least 42 young people* (of uncertain age, but old enough to know who he was and realize what that meant) insulted and jeered at him for whatever reason – maybe they were challenging his honor (in other words, according to the customs of the day, they were challenging him to defend himself and his reputation as a prophet – maybe even accusing him of lying about Elijah's ascension, and denying his status as a prophet), or maybe they were just looking for trouble. Elisha sees a threat. He asks God to deliver a just punishment. And that's what happened.

If that happened to you, I'll bet your shorts would be in a wad, too.

Read More!

<http://www.christian-thinktank.com/qmeanelisha.html>
<http://www.tektonics.org/af/callahanproph.html>

Chapter 25:

Daniel Doings

The book of Daniel contains some of the best examples of fulfilled prophecy in the Bible. To get around this, some critics try to date Daniel very late – to a time *after* all the events it predicts take place, into the second century before Christ (BC).

Do the arguments they make for doing this succeed? Let's look at some of them.

#1: Bouncin' Out Belshazzar

This first argument is kind of funny, because many years ago, the book of Daniel was criticized for claiming Belshazzar existed at all! It used to be argued that Belshazzar was a person Daniel just made up. Now that other documents have proven that he existed, the argument is that Daniel describes him he wrong way.

Daniel says that Belshazzar was a king, and a son of Nebuchadnezzar, a previous king. Critics think Daniel is wrong on both counts: They say he was just a *regent* (acting for his father, the real king), not an actual king, and that he was the son of another king, Nabodinus.

The first part is easy to answer. Documents show that Belshazzar acted as a king would and one even refers to him as bringing a sacrifice as "an offering of the king." Also, a Greek history of the fall of Babylon by Xenophon refers to him as king. Finally, even without all of this, Hebrew did not have a word for what Belshazzar would have been technically called otherwise (a "crown prince") so it makes sense that they'd call him a "king" instead, since that is what he acted as.

For the second part, there are a couple of answers possible. One is that "son" means "successor in king-ship," which is a use of the word "son" we know from other documents of the time (even when the successor was not a literal son). Another is that

Belshazzar was actually Nebuchadnezzar's grandson (the word used can also mean that), and we have some evidence that this was true. Another very good possibility is that Daniel was being sarcastic: Kings often falsely claimed to be related to prior kings, as a way of making it seem like they had earned the throne rightfully. Belshazzar and his father seem to have been usurpers (they took the throne illegitimately) so they may have either made up or exaggerated a family connection to Nebuchadnezzar. In that case, Daniel calls Belshazzar "son" because he is being sarcastic.

By the way, the fact that Belshazzar is mentioned is actually proof that Daniel was written early, because later historians seem to have forgotten he existed!

#2: Mede Minders

Another person Daniel is said to have made up is Darius the Mede. Unlike Belshazzar, we haven't found a clear reference to this person in other documents, and so to this day Daniel is accused of either making him up or confusing him with someone else.

Scholars have come up with two possible answers. One is that Darius is to be identified with a guy named Gubaru, who was the governor of Babylon under the Persians after they took over. Another is that Darius is another name for Cyrus the Persian, who is recognized as the person who took over the Babylonian Empire when the Persians invaded. There are detailed arguments for both ideas, but the second option equating Darius with Cyrus seems to be stronger.

One objection to these arguments is that no king – whether Gubaru or Cyrus – would have issued an edict like the one Daniel describes, forbidding people to pray to anyone but the king. But we need to keep in mind that the entire purpose of the edict was to trap Daniel. It is doubtful that the officials who presented it to Darius cared about whether anyone else obeyed it, and Darius would trust his advisors when they said it was something the people as a whole wanted. (It may have been something they wanted anyway: The prior rulers of Babylon had had some questionable religious ideas, and Darius may have had the edict presented this to him as a way of keeping order in a time of religious uncertainty.)

#3: Babylonian Spelling Bee

Here's one argument that has a funny answer. Some say that Daniel shows evidence of being written late because it spells the name of King Nebuchadnezzar wrong: It is supposed to be *-rezzar*, not *–nezzar*.

This is not much of an argument, because Jeremiah 27:9 also spells the name "wrong" and no one says Jeremiah was written late. It is spelled "wrong" in other places in the Old Testament too: 2 Kings, Chronicles, Ezra, Nehemiah, and Esther.

Even so, it probably isn't even a mistake. It was common and acceptable in the ancient Hebrew language to change an *r* to an *n* when spelling. However, there was probably a specific reason for the "wrong" spelling: The "correct" *-rezzar* spelling is a Hebrew version of the original name, *nabu-*

kudurru-usur, which means, "Nabu protect(s) the eldest son" (Nabu being a Babylonian god). The -*nezzar* spelling used in the Old Testament *may* be an adaptation from a pun made by Jewish opposition groups, *nabu-kudanu-usur* - which translates, "Nabu protect(s) the mule"!

#4: Mad Nebucadnezzar!

Critics also point to the story of Nebuchadnezzar's madness in Daniel 4. Critics claim that if this had really happened, Nebuchadnezzar would have been overthrown. But that's not necessarily true: Ancient people looked upon the insane as having been touched by the gods. If anything, an insane king may have been seen as a blessing to be cherished and protected at all costs.

At the same time, it is objected that there's no record of Nebuchadnezzar going mad outside of this record in Daniel. That's not entirely true: The Jewish historian Josephus says that it happened (though of course it is claimed that he's just using the Old Testament as a source). In addition, at least one Babylonian text seems to refer to Nebuchadnezzar having some sort of mental disorder. But we wouldn't expect this to necessarily be recorded by the Babylonians anyway, because as we said when it came to Akhenaten, anything that could be read in a bad way might not be recorded or could be destroyed later. (They probably didn't want their enemies learning about it, even if they thought it was a blessing to have him that way!)

#5: Watch Your Language!

The language of the book of Daniel causes a lot of arguments – not because of curse words or anything like that, but because some of the words it uses don't seem to belong. There are four language issues:

a) **Greek**. Daniel uses some Greek words – three of them, actually! – which critics think proves it had to be written later than the actual time of Daniel. But all three Greek words refer to musical instruments, and there was plenty of trade between the Greeks and the Babylonians.
b) **Persian**. Daniel uses several Persian words, but this is hardly an argument for a late date, because Daniel lived into the time when Persia took over Babylon, and most of the Persian words used are governmental terms, which makes sense if Daniel served in the government under the Persians.
c) **Aramaic**. Daniel is written partly in Aramaic, partly in Hebrew. Critics used to say that the Aramaic of Daniel was a form used in the second century BC, but detailed study has shown that it is actually in a form of Aramaic used in the fifth century BC, which is the time of the historical Daniel. (Of course, some critics just make the excuse that the earlier form of the Aramaic was preserved, just in Daniel, until the second century BC!)
d) **Hebrew**. Some also claim that the Hebrew of Daniel is a late form, but Hebrew changed

very slowly over time, so the evidence for this claim is ambiguous at best.

#6: The Four Kingdoms

To date Daniel late, critics have to interpret the four kingdoms in Daniel a certain way, like this:

- Kingdom #1= Babylonian empire
- Kingdom #2=Median empire
- Kingdom #3=Persian empire
- Kingdom #4=Greek empire

In history, the Medes and Persians were one kingdom together, but the critics need for Daniel to think of them as separate empires, because otherwise Daniel would have to be admitted to have made some accurate predictions even about times *after* the middle of the second century, and then there's no reason to date it late in the first place. (The fourth kingdom is actually Rome.)

But it's real hard to argue that a second-century author would have made such a mistake. People in the time of the second century knew that the Medes and Persians were a single empire. And the book of Daniel itself specifically says the Medes and Persians are partners, as in Daniel 5:28 when it says that Babylon was "given over to the Medes *and* Persians" and Daniel 6:8 which says "in accordance with the laws of the Medes and Persians...."

Read More!

<http://www.tektonics.org/af/danieldefense.html>

Chapter 26:

Slave Drivers, Part 1

The Old Testament gives instructions for how to buy and treat slaves. But isn't slavery a terrible thing? Why would God allow it and even explain how to manage it?

Before we answer that, we need to ask a question: What *is* slavery?

The problem is that "slavery" is used to describe a lot of different things, including the sort of slavery America used to have. But what we call "slavery" in the Old Testament isn't really anything like American slavery. (Slavery in the New Testament is another matter, but that's for another chapter.) And the word for "slave" in the Old Testament and in other documents from that time doesn't mean the same thing it would to us. We wouldn't say that the President's Cabinet members were his slaves, but they would have been called his "slaves" by people in the ancient world at the time of Moses. For what we find in the

Old Testament, it is better to use the word "servant" which simply means "someone who takes orders from someone else," than it is to use "slave".

A very important difference between what we call "slavery" and Old Testament "slavery" is that while most of the slaves we know of were kidnapped and made slaves against their will, Old Testament servants became servants of their own free will, usually to pay off debts. In this way, what the Bible describes is more like what we call "indentured servitude" – which is a way many free people came to America and paid their way here, when the country first started. (The sort of slavery America had was forbidden by the Old Testament: see Exodus 21:16 and Deut. 24:7.)

The Old Testament had many laws designed to help people so that they would not have to become servants like this. For example, it commanded that when money is lent to the poor, they are not to be charged interest. (This is a huge thing, because in other countries around Israel, high interest was the main reason people had to sell themselves into servitude.) Also, debts were supposed to be forgiven every seven years. But there were probably still times when people got in such terrible messes that becoming servants of others (or having family members become servants of others) was the only option – just as today, even though we have so many ways to help people, there are still always people who end up homeless.

Another important difference is that the Old Testament requires servants to be treated well. In fact, a master who killed a servant was given the death penalty, which would have never happened under American slavery. (The Old Testament does permit servants to be beaten with rods, but in that time, free people could be beaten with rods, too; for example, teachers sometimes beat students!)

There are many more differences between Old Testament "slavery" and what we call slavery, but those are two of the most important. To sum it up, though, Old Testament "slavery" was designed to help people in the greatest need – whereas American slavery was designed to exploit others.

Read More!

<http://www.christian-thinktank.com/qnoslave.html>

Chapter 27:

Flat Earth, Solid Sky

One of the oldest charges made against the Bible is that it teaches "bad cosmology" (teachings about the universe) – a flat earth and a solid sky. That's not what it does teach, but we'll need to explain something before we explain what it *does* teach.

Until modern times, most people would have no way to know anything about the shape of the earth or the nature of the sky. But they believed, mostly, that the earth was flat and the sky was solid.

Now let's say the Bible flatly stated that the earth was round and that the sky was not solid. What would most of the people who read or heard that, until recently, have thought?

To answer that question, here's an analogy: What would we think of a person who started talking about "glep plants" on "the planet Glorp" which was "around Alpha Centauri"? We'd think they were crazy. But what if we discovered 250 years from now that this person was right, that such things really did exist where he said? Well, that's fine for people living 250 years from now, but what good is that today? People will still think that person is crazy for the next 249 years.

In light of this, when God inspired the authors of the Bible, He made a wise choice: When it came to things like the shape of the earth, He had them use *equivocal* language. What this means is that you could understand it whether you believed the earth was flat or round – however you wanted to. The problem is that an *explicit* statement that

the earth was round would have offended countless people who believed that the earth was flat – so it is best to say nothing certain on the subject, which is exactly what happens in the Bible.

It should also be understood that the Hebrews, like all ancient cultures, obviously didn't have the scientific terminology we use to describe things today. We should not expect descriptions of "tectonic plates" or of "molten lava". In addition, we should expect many examples of "phenomenological" language – such as, *sunset*, *sunrise*, or references to sun and stars moving. As we still use such terms today, in spite of hundreds of years of knowing better, it should not reflect badly upon the use of such language in the Bible.

Now let's look at some of the actual Biblical passages and what kinds of language are used. I need to use the King James Version here because it is the words used by King James that sometimes cause the arguments.

#1: "Stretched" heavens

> Jer. 10:12 He hath made the earth by his power, he hath established the world by his wisdom, and hath stretched out the heavens by his discretion.

It is supposed that the use of the words like "stretched" or "expanse" indicates a physical dome. But this language is actually equivocal. The Hebrews (like many cultures of this time) lacked a word for infinite physical space. With that in mind, we may ask how they would describe the sky as it exists. We think that the sky as a "stretched" space or object comes as close to capturing "infinity" as one can without the word actually being used. And of course, they also would have no word for "gas" or "oxygen" so that sort of word would also probably be used to describe something like our atmosphere.

#2: Circle the Earth

> Is. 40:22 It is he that sitteth upon the **circle** of the earth, and the inhabitants thereof are as grasshoppers; that stretcheth out the heavens as a curtain, and spreadeth them out as a tent to dwell in...

Critics will assume that what is described is a flat, circular, pancake-like earth. But Hebrew had no special word for "sphere" – which is a three-dimensional circle. So "circle" here is an equivocal word that can mean a flat circle or a sphere.

#3 End of the World

> Job 28:24 For he looketh to the ends of the earth, and seeth under the whole heaven...

When the Bible refers to the "ends" of the earth, it is supposed that the author is thinking of opposite ends of a flat earth. But the word for "end" is used in many ways throughout the Old Testament. When used of geography, it can refer to the borders of a country or city. Then there's the word for "earth," which is used over 2500 times in the Old Testament. It can be used to mean the whole of the creation, but it is also used to refer to limited areas of land, such as a single country. So this is also equivocal language, and it cannot be said to teach a flat earth. (We might add that even today, knowing the world is a sphere, we use the phrase "ends of the earth" to refer to far away places!)

#4: Into the Corner

> Is. 11:12 And he shall set up an ensign for the nations, and shall assemble the outcasts of Israel, and gather together the dispersed of Judah from the four corners of the earth.

Some will say this as evidence that the Bible teaches a flat, *square* earth - which is a little odd, after it is argued so often that a flat, *circular* earth is what it teaches! But the word used actually refers to compass points – which we still use today.

#5: Lay a Foundation

> Ps. 104:5 Who laid the foundations of the earth, that it should not be removed for ever.

Passages that use the word "foundations" (or "pillars") are claimed to teach that the earth is flat and supported by pillars. Of course it never gets that specific, so this too is equivocal language.

#6: Jesus' Temptation

> Matthew 4:8 Again, the devil taketh him up into an exceeding high mountain, and sheweth him all the kingdoms of the world, and the glory of them...

It is often argued that this must teach a flat earth – and a mountain large enough to see it all! — because otherwise, Jesus could not have seen all the kingdoms of the world. But this is far too much to read into this verse. It is hardly likely that Matthew thought such a mountain existed, because it would obviously be visible from the low ground as well! In addition, Jesus and Satan being "supernatural" beings would not even need a mountain to see everything. It is clear that the trip to the mountain was just a way to try to tempt Jesus to power by putting him in a superior position over others – and that the vision of the kingdoms of the world was accomplished by some other miraculous means, not by direct vision. (Also, the word used for "world" in Luke's version just means the Roman Empire, while the word used in Matthew is sometimes used to mean the "world order.")

#7: Reaching Heaven

> Genesis 11:4 And they said, Go to, let us build us a city and a tower, whose top may reach unto heaven; and let us make us a name, lest we be scattered abroad upon the face of the whole earth.

This verse was once popular among critics, but not much any more. The words "may reach" are an insertion of the King James Version. This is now recognized as meaning that the tower was to be *dedicated* unto heaven, not built to reach it. Of course, even if it did have the other meaning, it only reflects what men "said" at the time — not that they were right about what they said.

Read More!

<http://www.tektonics.org/af/earthshape.html>

Chapter 28:

Doesn't Like Girls, Part 1

Some critics say the Bible takes a pretty dim view of women. Or even hates them. That's a pretty serious claim to make about half the human race.

We'll look at New Testament passages about this subject later, but what about some of the Old Testament passages used to argue this? Here are some examples I've heard.

#1: "The Bible says women are property." For example:

> Exodus 20:17 You shall not covet your neighbor's house. You shall not covet your neighbor's wife, or his manservant or maidservant, his ox or donkey, or anything that belongs to your neighbor.

This verse is sometimes used to claim that the Bible sees women as nothing but the property of men. The argument is that a wife is listed along with other forms of property, such as slaves and animals.

In the chapter titled "Slave Drivers, Part 1" we pointed out that these servants were not considered property, but even if they were, this would be one of those logical fallacies we talked about in the first chapter. (For fun, see if you can decide which one.) The critic assumes that the subject of the sentence is, "property you shouldn't covet" – that because a couple of things listed are "property," everything else on the list is too. But there's no reason to assume that. This is like arguing that because your shopping list says, "bread, tuna, corn, floor cleaner," you think floor cleaner is something you can eat. The list's topic is just, "that which you should not covet" – it doesn't say it is all property.

#2: "The Bible says only men can serve as priests. That means women didn't have access to God." If this is true, then it seems strange that there are so many examples of women who are shown talking to God without a man around. Hagar, Leah, Rachel, Deborah, Hannah, Huldah and others spoke to God one on one – they didn't ask for a man to come make the call.

Of course, we can agree that only men were priests. But women are shown doing everything else associated with the worship of God. They brought the same sacrifices. They made the same vows. Some became prophets. You may still say that it is unfair that women couldn't become priests, but the likely reason this happened is because pagan religions of the time used female priests and they were associated with sexual worship practices. Other practices in the Old Testament religion were designed to work against temptations to this kind of worship (for example, the robes of the priests did not open from the front!), so this is not "anti-woman" – it is "anti-pagan."

#3: "God is always said to be male!" This is not true. God is described with feminine imagery in several places, such as in Deuteronomy 32:18: "You deserted the Rock, who fathered you; you forgot the God who gave you birth." Male imagery is used more often, but ancient people used gender language to describe their gods because of the way they related to the universe and to people, not because they assigned the gods real gender.

#4: "God said that a woman is 'unclean' twice as long if she gives birth to a girl!" This is true. It's in Leviticus 12:1-5:

> The LORD said to Moses, "Say to the Israelites: 'A woman who becomes pregnant and gives birth to a son will be ceremonially unclean for seven days, just as she is unclean during her monthly period. On the eighth day the boy is to be circumcised. Then the woman must wait thirty-three days to be purified from her bleeding. She must not touch anything sacred or go to the sanctuary until the days of her purification are over. If she gives birth to a daughter, for two weeks the woman will be unclean, as during her period. Then she must wait sixty-six days to be purified from her bleeding.'"

But remember from the chapter, "Reading Leviticus Can be Fun" that "unclean" does not mean dirty or bad. It also doesn't imply that a boy and girl are unequal in value because in the next verse (v. 6) it says that parents of any baby born (boy **or** girl) must bring the same offering, which is a year-old lamb. And if anything, Leviticus 12:1-5 is biased *for* girls, because the girl gets to spend more time bonding with her mother than the boy does.

#5: "There's a real weird ritual in Numbers 5 women had to go through!" It seems weird to us, but that doesn't mean it was to them. But regardless of that, we have to know more about the background (just like in the chapter on Leviticus) to understand that this ritual was actually meant to help women, not hurt them.

The ritual went like this. A man who accused his wife of cheating on him could bring her to the priest, where he would give her a cup of water with some dust in it to drink and have her take an oath that she hadn't cheated. If she was lying, she would get really sick. If she was telling the truth, she wouldn't.

Sounds weird and unfair? Not really. For one thing, since this was a public proclamation, the husband would be humiliated if he wasn't telling the truth (and remember what we said in the chapter "Culture Shock" about how people in this time felt about being humiliated or shamed). Also, in the other nations around Israel, women didn't even have a chance to clear their name like they did in this test. If a husband said his wife cheated on him, he could kill her – no questions asked. Or, women suspected of cheating were thrown in the river, and if they were guilty, it was assumed they would drown! (Keep in mind they didn't have swimming lessons back then.)

It'd be a good idea to check out any claims you here that the Old Testament is "anti-woman." It definitely isn't.

Read More!

<http://www.christian-thinktank.com/femalex.html>

Chapter 29:

Number Crunch

Numbers are all over the Bible. No, not the book of Numbers, where they counted people a lot. I mean like 1, 2, 3…you do the rest, and let me know when you're done. And if you need a break while doing that, check out a few of the arguments I've seen over the years about numbers in the Bible.

#1: A Pi in the Face. 1 Kings 7:23 says:

> He made the Sea of cast metal, circular in shape, measuring ten cubits from rim to rim and five cubits high. It took a line of thirty cubits to measure around it.

There were once some egghead critics who checked this out, and when they were finished, they said, "Ahhhh, ha ha ha ha. This verse gives an inaccurate value for pi. Ha ha."

What's that all about? You may not remember from math class (who would?), but pi is the value which is, "the ratio of the circumference of a circle to its diameter." That ratio is an infinite number which begins 3.14159...and continues on forever, as far as we know.

Now the eggheads looked at "ten cubits" and "thirty cubits" and said, "That wouldn't make a ratio equal to pi. The Bible's wrong. Ha ha." (The eggheads don't have much of a life.)

Well, there are a lot of answers to this. One is that the bath just wasn't a perfect circle. (It's not like they had laser levels or stuff like that.) The more common answer is that 1 Kings 7:23 is rounding off the measurements. This makes sense, for several reasons. First, ancient writers almost always rounded off figures, unless they were mathematics experts (which the author of 1 Kings probably wasn't). Second, since pi goes on forever, *any* expression of it is an estimate. Third, we don't consider estimates to be mistakes in everyday writing. Put it this way: If we ask how many gallons of fuel a rocket contains, we expect a detailed answer like "4,942,827.78 gallons" from a NASA engineer, if he is involved in a technical discussion with other engineers. If he's talking to the press, and he is savvy, he'll say "4.9 million gallons" rather than bewilder the reporters with more detail. Your average hobbyist (or even a reporter) will say "5 million gallons." Are any of them incorrect? No, because there is an assumption that you'll be more precise the more of an expert you are. Unless the Bible authors were mathematicians on the level of Archimedes (he was an ancient guy who went real far in deciding the value of pi) then we should expect them to round off numbers.

#2: Take Two Thousand Baths. Speaking of baths, here's another good one, and it's actually one of many such examples in the Bible:

> 1 Kings 7:26 It was a handbreadth in thickness, and its rim was like the rim of a cup, like a lily blossom. It held two thousand baths.
>
> 2 Chronicles 4:5 It was a handbreadth in thickness, and its rim was like the rim of a cup, like a lily blossom. It held three thousand baths.

These two verses are obviously talking about the same container. But did it hold 2000 baths, or 3000? I'll explain the answer by another example not from the Bible.

Let's say the works of one ancient historian of Rome contain a known error in numbering which has been faulted to a mistake made not by the historian when he wrote, but to someone who copied his work later. Two places are described as being 25 miles apart. But we know that the locations are actually *125* miles apart, not 25.

Most scholars would say, "Oh, that's easy. When it was copied, someone made a mistake. In Roman numerals, the historian wrote CXXV. But someone forgot to copy the C, so that it now says XXV."

In the same way, someone who copied either Kings or Chronicles –we don't know who or when – mistook a 2 for a 3, or the other way around.

Answers like this are not a stretch of the imagination. Scholars who work with the Bible and other ancient texts often find places where things were copied wrong, and as it happens, numbers are one of the things that are most often messed up.

#3: The Big Quail Bar-B-Q. One last sample, from the book of – um, Numbers. And I have to use King James for this one since it is what the critics use.

> Numbers 11:31-2 And there went forth a wind from the LORD, and brought quails from the sea, and let them fall by the camp, as it were a day's journey on this side, and as it were a day's journey on the other side, round about the camp, and as it were two cubits high upon the face of the earth. And the people stood up all that day, and all that night, and all the next day, and they gathered the quails: he that gathered least gathered ten homers: and they spread them all abroad for themselves round about the camp.

"Homers" (I wonder if they also had a unit of measure called, "Simpsons"?) were pretty big. We're not sure how big. But one of the eggheads who is a critic says that this means that the Israelites gathered over **29 trillion** quail! That's a lot of barbeque sauce!

Unfortunately, he made two big mistakes. For one thing, he assumed that "the people" means *every single Israelite* (there were maybe 2 million on the Exodus) when in fact no number is given. "The people" just means whoever went out – like we say, "there are people at the race today." We don't know the number, but according to Numbers 11:4, it was the few non-Israelites who started the complaining about there being no meat, so there were probably one a few people who went out to collect quail. Second, he read the King James as saying that the quail were three feet **deep** on the ground. But the grammar can be read as indicating that this was the *height* at which the birds were flying when they were caught or knocked down. We don't know how many quail were actually caught, then.

That's just three examples of what happens when some critics "play the numbers" in the Bible.

Read More!

<http://www.tektonics.org/lp/piwrong.html>
<http://wwww.tektonics.org/af/copyisterrors.html>
<http://www.tektonics.org/af/exoduslogistic.html>

Chapter 30:

Common Census, Part 1

Here's a question. 2 Samuel 24 says that God moved David to take a census of Israel, but 1 Chronicles 21 says that Satan moved David to do it. So who did what?

The first point we need to make is that nothing forbids God from using the wicked to serve His purposes. In the Bible, He used the pagan Babylonian army as a judgment weapon on Israel, and used a "lying spirit" to deceive King Ahab. So there's no reason why He can't use Satan for His own purposes too.

Second, the book of Job tells us that Satan tries to get God to allow harm to come to His people. In 2 Samuel 24, God is said to be angry with Israel. This would have been just the time when Satan would stand to accuse Israel of sin and say that they should be punished.

Someone might say this is just a strained answer for an obvious contradiction. But the fact is that the

Bible does present us with a concept called *dual agency* – in which more than one party can be said to be responsible for an action, without mentioning more than one of them. For example, Numbers 13:1 says God told Moses to send spies into Canaan, but Deut. 1:22 has Moses saying that the Israelites requested this. The reason for the difference is that the sending of the spies was something the people committed a sin over, so Deuteronomy purposely shifts responsibility for what happened, to the people, who agreed to send the spies at God's command.

Read More!

<http://www.christian-thinktank.com/hcensus.html>

Chapter 31:

Has Tyre Gone Flat?

In Ezekiel 26:3-20 there's a prophecy of what will happen to the ancient city of Tyre. A lot of Christians think this is a very good example of how the Bible has made accurate prophecies.

Of course there are some people who disagree, which is why we're here.

One of the first things we need to look at is a claim that though the prophecy was fulfilled, it was by the wrong people, so the Bible is wrong. We say that verses 3-5 and then 12-20 refer to stuff done by Nebuchadnezzar, the king of Babylon, while verses 6-11 refer to stuff done by Alexander the Great, a Greek king who came later. The doubters say that no, the Bible means for us to understand that Nebuchadnezzar was supposed to do everything between verses 3 and 20.

Let's look at each of those verses and figure out what they mean, and who is supposed to be doing what. I'll use King James again here, because it's clearer in this case.

3 *Therefore thus saith the Lord GOD; Behold, I am against thee, O Tyrus, and will cause many nations to come up against thee, as the sea causeth his waves to come up*. Notice who is said to be in charge. It is the Lord God who will "cause many nations" to come up. The use of the Hebrew word Adonai (which means *sovereign* or *controller*) places God at the head of the nations. At this point "the nations" can mean any nation at all. That includes Babylon and also Greece.

No one can dispute that a lot of nations came against Tyre. Babylon was the first of these. Alexander the Great was next, and he had a whole group of Greek city-states represented with him. Each of these was an independent entity and acted as a nation unto itself. Alexander also had help from a lot of other nations that were not Greek, such as Phoenicia and Lycia.

4 *And they shall destroy the walls of Tyrus, and break down her towers: I will also scrape her dust from her, and make her like the top of a rock.* It's still God ("I") in charge, and He's in charge of the nations. So it is the nations who will scrape Tyre off,

and destroy the walls, and break down the towers. Any nations, not just one.

It's hard to argue that this didn't happen. There were two parts to Tyre, one on the mainland and one on an island not far from the shore. Nebuchadnezzar defeated the part on the mainland and by the time of Alexander it was just a bunch of rubble. Alexander used that rubble to make a bridge to the island part of the city and defeat it. By doing this he "scraped the dust" away and made the place of the mainland city "like the top of a rock" – bare.

5 It shall be a place for the spreading of nets in the midst of the sea: for I have spoken it, saith the Lord GOD: and it shall become a spoil to the nations. The "spoil to the nations" part is easy. Both Nebuchadnezzar and Alexander took spoils from their conquests. That was normal in war back then. The "fishnets" part, like any private action by a single person like a peasant fisherman, is not something we can prove happened, any more than we can prove that they ate eggs for breakfast on June the first, but it's not something that would **not** happen by the coast in an area with plenty of room.

6 And her daughters which are in the field shall be slain by the sword; and they shall know that I am the LORD. 7 For thus saith the Lord GOD; Behold, I will bring upon Tyrus Nebuchadrezzar king of Babylon, a king of kings, from the north, with horses, and with chariots, and with horsemen, and companies, and much people. God now is said to bring on a specific attacker: Nebuchadnezzar. This brings the *first* of the nations against Tyre. Now notice how the pairing changes:

8 He shall slay with the sword thy daughters in the field: and he shall make a fort against thee, and cast a mount against thee, and lift up the buckler against thee. Notice that now the pairing I/they is not used, but it is now *he* – Nebuchadnezzar, not God — who is "in charge" of the scene. It is he and his army who are the ones who act – not God and the nations.

9 And he shall set engines of war against thy walls, and with his axes he shall break down thy towers. 10 By reason of the abundance of his horses their dust shall cover thee: thy walls shall shake at the noise of the horsemen, and of the wheels, and of the chariots, when he shall enter into thy gates, as men enter into a city wherein is made a breach. 11 With the hoofs of his horses shall he tread down all thy streets: he shall slay thy people by the sword, and thy strong garrisons shall go down to the ground.

The use of "he" and "his" continues in these verses, which all agree refer to Nebuchadnezzar and which no one thinks was not fulfilled in history. But watch out for the change in this next set of verses:

*12 And they shall make a spoil of thy riches, and make a prey of thy merchandise: and they shall break down thy walls, and destroy thy pleasant houses: and they shall lay thy stones and thy timber and thy dust in the midst of the water. 13 And I will cause the noise of thy songs to cease; and the sound of thy harps shall be no more heard. 14 And **I** will make thee like the top of a rock: thou shalt be a place to* *spread nets upon; thou shalt be built no more: for I the LORD have spoken it, saith the Lord GOD.*

It's not "he" or "his" any more. We're back to "they" and "I" (as in God). So this means that the events described in verses 12-14 could be done by any of the "nations" that attacked Tyre, including Alexander's Greek army – and no one disputes that Alexander was the one that threw the stones and timber of the mainland city into the water. That means that there can be no argument that Nebuchadnezzar was the only one who could have done what was described in verses 12-14 for the prophecy to be fulfilled.

There's one other issue to mention. Verse 14 says Tyre will be "built no more" and some people say that this isn't true because there's a city called Tyre today. But aside from the fact that it isn't in the same spot, and has nothing in common with the ancient city except a name, there's no need to think that Ezekiel's word don't allow Tyre to come back again *ever*. The reason for this is that ancient people used language a lot differently than we do sometimes, especially when it came to talking about war. For example, remember how we saw in another chapter how an Egyptian pharaoh said some people were "made non-existent" and then said he captured them. How can he capture people who don't exist? The answer is that words like "made non-existent" aren't meant literally but were kind of like what we call "trash talk" that we hear at sports events. So when Ezekiel says that Tyre will be "built no more" but is saying, "Guys, you're gonna lose BAD!"

Read More!

<http://www.tektonics.org/uz/zeketyre.html>
<http://www.apologeticspress.org/articles/254?>

The New Testament

Whew. We're done with the Old Testament. Now for the New Testament. I know you have a lot more questions about this part. Right?

Chapter 32:

No Jesus, No Piece!

You might be used to people saying Jesus never did miracles, never rose from the dead, or even never said half the things the New Testament said he did. But things are getting so desperate for some critics that they now even want to argue that *Jesus didn't exist at all.*

You might think that this is the sort of idea that is found in those kooky newspapers you see at the grocery store with headlines like *Bigfoot Crashes Wine Tasting Party.* And in a way, that's true. The people who say this are not historians – that is, people with credentials in history. They're one of two things: Either people with education in a subject other than history, or else people with no real education at all (that is, no education, or only limited education in history).

This doesn't mean scholars are always right. But it does mean that if you want to argue against what the smartest and most informed people say in a subject they're good at, you're going to need some mighty good arguments. And that's exactly what "Christ mythers" (people who say Jesus never existed) do **not** have. In fact, Christ mythers often rely on stretching the truth and leaving out important facts.

Let's look at an example of that right now. In the middle of the second century, a Christian named Justin Martyr wrote about a conversation he had with a Jewish person named Trypho. Here is a part of that conversation that Christ mythers often quote:

> When I had said this, my beloved friends, those who were with Trypho laughed; but he, smiling, says, "I approve of your other remarks, and admire the eagerness with which you study divine things; but it were better for you still to abide in the philosophy of Plato, or of some other man, cultivating endurance, self-control, and moderation, rather than be deceived by false words, and follow the opinions of men of no reputation. For if you

remain in that mode of philosophy, and live blamelessly, a hope of a better destiny were left to you; but when you have forsaken God, and reposed confidence in man, what safety still awaits you? If, then, you are willing to listen to me (for I have already considered you a friend), first be circumcised, then observe what ordinances have been enacted with respect to the Sabbath, and the feasts, and the new moons of God; and, in a word, do all things which have been written in the law: and then perhaps you shall obtain mercy from God. But **Christ—if He has indeed been born, and exists anywhere—is unknown, and does not even know Himself, and has no power until Elias come to anoint Him, and make Him manifest to all. And you, having accepted a groundless report, invent a Christ for yourselves**, and for his sake are inconsiderately perishing."

The Christ mythers say that it was Jesus who was "made" and who was "entirely unknown." But the context makes it clear that Trypho is not referring to the man Jesus. Trypho takes Jesus' existence for granted throughout the debate with Justin. Look what else he says in the same conversation:

- xxxii – "...But this so-called Christ of yours *was dishonourable and inglorious*, so much so that *the last curse contained in the law of God fell on him, for he was crucified.*"

- xxvi –"Now show if *this man* be He of whom these prophecies were made."
- xxxviii – "For you utter many blasphemies, in that you seek to persuade us that this crucified man was with Moses and Aaron, and spoke to them in the pillar of the cloud; then that he *became man, was crucified,* and ascended up to heaven, and comes again to earth, and ought to be worshipped."
- xxxxix — And Trypho said, "Those who affirm him to have been a man, and to have been anointed by election, and then to have become Christ, appear to me to speak more plausibly than you who hold those opinions which you express. For we all expect that Christ will be a man [born] of men, and that Elijah when he comes will anoint him. But if this man appear to be Christ, he must certainly be known as man [born] of men; but from the circumstance that Elijah has not yet come, I infer that this man is not He [the Christ]."

What Trypho means in his earlier statement is that the *Messiah* - which is to say, the position or "job" of the Messiah - has been created by the Christians: He is saying that the "Christ" has not come in Jesus, but that Christians have made Jesus a Christ for themselves, and if the true Messiah was born and lived somewhere, he is entirely unknown. There was a Jewish belief at this time that the Christ, when he came, would not proclaim himself, but would let others say who he was. Trypho is accusing the Christians of identifying one as Christ who is *not* Christ — he is not accusing them of making up a man of history.

"Hey, wait a minute. That's not good enough. If Jesus existed and was so famous, we should have heard a lot more about him besides what Christians said. In fact, here's a long list of writers who didn't mention Jesus! What do you think of THAT?"

Christ mythers like to pull out a long list of names of people back in Jesus' day (supposedly) who did not mention Jesus. If you ever see a list like this, it probably came originally from an author named John Remsberg. Remsberg wasn't a historian or an expert in history – he was a teacher and a superintendent of schools in the state of Kansas back in Theodore Roosevelt's time. (He is also vague about whether he is talking about Jesus existing only as a man, or as a miracle worker. But the response to him would be the same either way.)

There are a lot of problems with Remsberg's list. In some cases, an author he names really did mention Jesus (we'll look at two of them below), although he sometimes argued against the mention of Jesus being worthwhile. In some cases there's no clue who the person named is and what they wrote (as in, he gives a name, but it could be the name of several ancient people, because it is a name like "Smith" that a lot of people had). But in most cases, the people Remsberg named would never have any reason to mention Jesus in the first place, because they were writing about subjects that had nothing to do with Jesus. For example:

Arrian – he wrote a history of Alexander the Great, who was 300 years before Jesus! So what does Remsberg expect Arrian to say? "Alexander defeated the Persians. By the way, this has nothing to do with Jesus, who lived 300 years later."

Valerius Maximus – this guy wrote a book of stories for speakers to use, around 30 AD. In other words, he wrote the ancient equivalent to one of those desktop *Dilbert* calendars. Where would Jesus belong in that?

Columella — this guy wrote about agriculture and trees!

Statius — this guy was a poet who wrote the *Thebaid*, about the Seven against Thebes, the *Achilleid*, a life of Achilles, and a collection of poems called the *Silvae*. I see plenty of reason to mention Jesus, don't you?

Whenever a Christ myther claims that some writer didn't mention Jesus, there are two things you can ask: *First*, did this person ever write anything that would have had a reason to mention Jesus? *Second*, did this person ever write about other people similar to Jesus? For example, there were many other Jewish teachers and people who were supposed to have done miracles at the same time Jesus lived. There were teachers like the rabbis Gamaliel and Hillel and Shammai. There were miracle-workers like Honi the Circle Drawer and Hanina ben dosa. By the logic of the Christ myther, the fact that someone like Columella doesn't mention these people shows they didn't exist either.

But there' another question to ask: *Why would any of these writers mention Jesus anyway?* We have to understand why they would not, from **their** point of view. To someone like Columella or Statius, even if Jesus was someone within their topic, Jesus would not be seen as important. Obviously they would not believe he really did miracles, or if they did, they would say what a pagan guy named Celsus said later: That he got his power to do miracles from doing magic. Jesus did not address the Roman Senate, or write fancy works of philosophy. Jesus was also executed as a criminal, which would make him look very bad to a pagan. On top of all that, Jesus was poor, and lived out in the country – so the Roman writers would be too snobby to think he was worth talking about.

But that's not to say Jesus was never mentioned by any historians of his time. He was, but the Christ mythers have to come and fight about whether those historians are any good for showing Jesus existed. Let's talk about two of those historians who give the best evidence – Tacitus and Josephus.

Tacitus was a Roman historian who wrote around 110 AD (second century). He wrote about Jesus in his work called the *Annals*:

> But not all the relief that could come from man, not all the bounties that the prince could bestow, nor all the atonements which could be presented to the gods, availed to relieve

> Nero from the infamy of being believed to have ordered the conflagration, the fire of Rome. Hence to suppress the rumor, he falsely charged with the guilt, and punished Christians, who were hated for their enormities. **Christus, the founder of the name, was put to death by Pontius Pilate, procurator of Judea in the reign of Tiberius**: but the pernicious superstition, repressed for a time broke out again, not only through Judea, where the mischief originated, but through the city of Rome also, where all things hideous and shameful from every part of the world find their center and become popular. Accordingly, an arrest was first made of all who pleaded guilty; then, upon their information, an immense multitude was convicted, not so much of the crime of firing the city, as of hatred against mankind.

This seems pretty clear. How do the Christ mythers explain this one?

"It's a forgery! Some Christian fraud added it in later!"

That's not a very good reason, and it certainly isn't one the people who know the most about Tacitus would back up. It's written just the way Tacitus would write; it's found in every copy of the *Annals* we have from the earliest time (the 11th century); and it says such bad things about Christians that it's not likely a Christian would write it, unless you want to really get crazy and say some Christian purposely wrote bad things like that to fool us. And that would be *really* crazy – more than we can help you with.

"Tacitus wasn't reliable! He could have just put this down without looking into it."

No way. When it comes to accuracy, care, critical capability, and trustworthiness, the people who study Tacitus are unanimous: The man knew his business. They say he always did his research, and was good at it. He wasn't perfect, of course, but the point is that if you want to say he made a mistake here, *you're* the one who needs proof.

"Tacitus was biased!"

This is true, but it won't work because if Tacitus had any bias, it would be *against* Christians, not for them. Like most Romans, he didn't like Jewish people, and Jesus was Jewish. And anyway, the people who are experts on Tacitus say that even when he *was* biased, it never caused him to make up things.

"Tacitus called Pilate a 'procurator' but he was really a prefect. So he probably messed up when he thought Jesus existed too."

A procurator was someone who handled money matters, while a prefect was a military official. It's more likely that Pilate held both titles than that Tacitus made a mistake.

"Tacitus calls Jesus 'Christ' and not by a proper name. That wouldn't be right."

Why not? Tacitus would use the name his readers would know best, and that would not be the name that Jesus was executed under. By the time he was writing, 80 years after Jesus died, "Christus" was used as a proper name for Jesus. In fact, it is already used as a proper name by Paul only 20-30 years after Jesus died.

"Tacitus says there was a 'great multitude' of Christians at Rome. There wouldn't be this many Christians in Rome at this early time."

How many would that be? What does Tacitus mean here by a "great multitude"? 50? 100? 500? Is it a relative for, "a lot, considering the crime committed"? (If we arrested 50 people for holding up a corner gas station, does that seem like a "great multitude" to arrest for such a little crime?)

So Tacitus provides good evidence that Jesus existed, and all of the arguments against him fail. Now let's talk about Josephus. This guy was a Jewish historian who lived just after the time of Jesus, and he actually mentions Jesus in two places. Here's the first one, which we can call the "shorter" reference:

> Antiquities 20.9.1 But the younger Ananus who, as we said, received the high priesthood, was of a bold disposition and exceptionally daring; he followed the party of the Sadducees, who are severe in judgment above all the Jews, as we have already shown. As therefore Ananus was of such a disposition, he thought he had now a good opportunity, as Festus was now dead, and Albinus was still on the road; so he assembled a council of judges, and brought before it the brother of **Jesus the so-called Christ,** whose name was James, together with some others, and having

> accused them as law-breakers, he delivered them over to be stoned.

And here's the other, what we can call the "longer" reference:

> Antiquities 18.3.3 Now there was about this time **Jesus**, a wise man, if it be lawful to call him a man, for he was a doer of wonderful works, a teacher of such men as receive the truth with pleasure. He drew over to him both many of the Jews, and many of the Gentiles. He was the Christ, and when Pilate, at the suggestion of the principal men among us, had condemned him to the cross, those that loved him at the first did not forsake him; for he appeared to them alive again the third day; as the divine prophets had foretold these and ten thousand other wonderful things concerning him. And the tribe of Christians so named from him are not extinct at this day.

So, what do the Christ mythers say about these?

"They're a forgery! Some Christian fraud added them in later!"

This time when they say something like this, they actually have a point – for one of the two references. The shorter one they have no case against – it's in all the copies of Josephus we have, as is, and the scholars who know a lot about Josephus stand behind it completely. It uses a non-Christian term when it describes James as "brother of Jesus" (Christians liked to use "brother of the Lord" or "brother of the Savior" instead). It doesn't make a big deal about Jesus, but mentions Jesus in passing. It also doesn't connect Jesus with John the Baptist, as we would think a Christian would do if they added it in.

Some Christ mythers say the phrase "so-called Christ" is Christian because it is the same words used in Matthew 1:16. But Josephus uses the word for "so-called" in his writings elsewhere.

The larger quote is another story. On that one, we have some evidence from a copy of Josephus (one written in Arabic) as well as some historical and style issues. Let's look at that quote again, with some stuff highlighted:

> Antiquities 18.3.3 Now there was about this time Jesus, a wise man**, if it be lawful to call him a man**, for he was a doer of wonderful works, a teacher of such men as receive the truth with pleasure. He drew over to him both many of the Jews, and many of the Gentiles. **He was the Christ**, and when Pilate, at the suggestion of the principal men among us, had condemned him to the cross, those that loved him at the first did not forsake him; **for he appeared to them alive again the third day; as the divine prophets had foretold these and ten thousand other wonderful things concerning him**. And the tribe of Christians so named from him are not extinct at this day.

On this one, all the people who are experts in Josephus agree that there were *some* things added to this passage that should not be there. The stuff in bold they say definitely or very likely doesn't belong. But there's no argument from them against that Josephus did write most of this. The Christ mythers, of course, don't agree.

"Josephus would never say nice things about Jesus, like that he did wonderful works and was wise."

That's not true. Josephus could easily have admired Jesus as a teacher and a miracle worker, just as we might admire someone for doing charity work even if we don't agree with their politics. Even today there are many people who respect Jesus for his teachings but aren't Christians. There's even a group that exists today called Atheists for Jesus! So why couldn't Josephus have called Jesus a "wise man"?

There's also no reason Josephus could not have said that Jesus did miracles. Actually, he may not even be complimenting Jesus here because the word he uses can mean *strange*, *surprising*, or *wonderful.*

"It's out of context. Josephus is discussing Jewish troubles, and the longer passage is out of place. Without it, the text runs on in proper sequence."

This isn't much of an argument either. Experts on Josephus have called him a "patchwork writer" who jumps around a lot, so he doesn't always stick to his topics. Besides, look at what's covered around it:

- 18.35 Pilate arrives in Judea.

- 18.55-9 Pilate introduces imperial images in the Temple, causing a ruckus.
- 18.60-2 Pilate expropriates Temple funds to build an aqueduct.
- 18.63-4 The passage about Jesus.
- 18.65-80 An event set in Rome, not involving Pilate directly, having to do with the seduction of a follower of Isis in Rome.
- 18.81-4 An account of four Jewish scoundrels; also not directly involving Pilate.
- 18.85-7 An incident involving Pilate and some Samaritans.
- 18.88-9 Pilate gets the imperial boot.

This is in no way a set of connected events. Pilate has a part in all of them, but there's no other obvious connection that lets us say, "The one about Jesus is out of context."

That leaves one question: Why did Christians add in those things? Some Christ mythers say they were being dishonest, but there's no need to say that. You probably know how some people like to "argue" with books they read and scribble "replies" in the margins. The stuff that scholars think was added looks a lot like someone doing that.

Read More!

<http://www.tektonics.org/jesusexist/jesusexisthub.html>

James Patrick Holding, ed. *Shattering the Christ Myth* (Xulon Press), 2008.

Some of the people we have answers to, that you may encounter:

- G. A. Wells
- Earl Doherty

Chapter 33:

Jesus Came From a Ghost Town

These days, not only are some critics saying that Jesus didn't exist...they're saying the town he lived in (Nazareth) *didn't exist either*! It's not seen as often as the "Jesus myth" but in 2008 one guy wrote a whole book on it.

I answered that critic more fully in the book listed at the end of the last chapter. But here are two big pointers about the "Nazareth myth." (I learned a lot about this from a guy named Dr. James Strange, who's one of the leading experts on Nazareth. He's a really cool guy, by the way – he has a picture from the "Dr. Strange" comic book on his door. Just the kind of professor you'll wish you had in all your classes.)

#1: It's not honest about the evidence. It's claimed by Nazareth mythers that there's no archeological evidence for Nazareth at the time of Jesus. But that's just plain wrong. There's plenty of evidence for Nazareth at the time of Jesus (from what is called the "Early Roman" period), though not as much as we might find for other towns from the same time, because modern Nazareth is built right over the top of the place where the city Jesus lived in was. That means most of the evidence has been found in what are called "casual finds" – things found by people digging for other reasons, like construction, not by archaeologists doing scheduled digs. (That critic I refuted just dismissed this kind of evidence because he claimed archaeologists were careless or didn't know what they were doing.)

#2: It misreads the Bible. The "Nazareth mythers" like to say that there's no evidence for a town as big as Nazareth. They think the Bible reads Nazareth as some sort of large, urban metropolis because it uses the word *polis* to describe it. But despite what you may think from Superman comics ("Metropolis"), *polis* doesn't mean "big city." In fact, we're not sure what it meant or why it was applied to certain cities or villages people lived in.

You may hear more about this one in the future – but probably not as much as about the "Jesus myth."

Chapter 34:

Copycat, Copycat, Jesus is a *Copycat!*

There's a kind of argument out there that goes something like this...

"Jesus? He's no different than a million other gods like ______ who were also born of a

virgin, crucified, and rose from the dead. Big deal."

Now, you won't be likely to hear this from the *really* smart people with the big degrees. But you *will* find it in best-selling novels like *The Da Vinci Code* and also in books by people who should probably sell used cars instead of write books. They have a long list of names of gods they like to put in that blank, but we don't have a lot of room here, so we're just going to ask a few questions, then talk about three of the most common gods that are used to fill in the blank. Then, as always, there'll be a place you can go for more information.

Let's start with those questions. The first is *how do we really decide if something is a copy of something else?*

To use an example, if one of your professors says that you plagiarized someone else's work in a paper you turned in, what kind of proof should that professor have that you copied someone else, before you get a failing grade? What would show that you did *not* copy from someone else, and deserve to have your paper fairly evaluated like everyone else's?

In the same way, what kind of proof do we need to say that something about Jesus was

copied from another god?

Well, the first thing that obviously has to be true is that the pagan god had to have been known to exist *before* Jesus lived in the first century. This is important because, as we'll see in some of our examples, the evidence can show that the people who believed in the pagan god are the ones who changed the stories of their god to make him more like Jesus – because they were trying to compete with the Christians. In the same way, you can't be accused of plagiarizing a paper that you can show was written *after* yours.

Second, when someone says something is a copy of something else, it has to be shown that the thing copied was *unique* and not something that someone could come up with on their own, or that the type of thing they're writing about would naturally involve the same subject.

What I mean is this: You can't be accused of plagiarism if your paper uses words like *and, but, the,* and *also*. Those are words **everyone** uses. Also, you can't be accused of plagiarism if you are assigned to write a paper on hydroelectric power, and you happen to use some of the same arguments or facts about hydroelectric power as someone else does before you. That's because facts aren't the property of just one person. You can't be accused of plagiarism if you simply say that "dams are a source of hydroelectric power" the same as someone else did.

So for example, if someone says, "Jesus was a teacher" and then says, "_____ was a teacher", this isn't a good argument. Being a teacher is something **any** god would be expected to do. The same is true for doing miracles: Any god (real or imagined) would do them. If someone says, "Christians had a sacred meal (communion), so did this pagan religion", that doesn't prove copying, because in the ancient world a lot of groups had sacred meals together, just like families today like to go out to eat to enjoy each others' company.

Something has to be unique to make a charge of copying stick – such as if your professor finds that you have a whole paragraph in your paper that is *exactly the same words* as someone else's, not just the same subject. It's not plagiarism to say, as someone else did, the fact that dams create hydroelectric power; but it *is* plagiarism to say it using someone else's exact words and not giving them credit for it.

What it boils down to is, you can't yell "Copycat!" unless you can show that there's no other explanation than that someone copied someone else. But now let's look at some of those gods it is said that Christians copied from to make Jesus. What we'll find is that in most cases, the claim that a pagan god did something like Jesus is actually *false* – completely made up! In the next greater number of cases, the information about the pagan god comes from a time *after* Jesus lived, which means if anyone copied anyone, it was pagans who copied Christians, not the other way around. Finally, we'll see that nearly all of the rest are things that are not unique or special, so that like using the words *but* and *the* in a class paper, it doesn't really mean anything.

Attis, the Deity Who Had an Unkind Cut

Have you ever heard of Attis? Probably not. But he did have a religion about him in Rome about the time Jesus was alive. What are some of the things you might hear about this guy? Here's a list of some of the most important:

Attis was born on December 25th of the Virgin Nana.

First of all, we can forget about the Dec. 25th part. Although we do celebrate Jesus' birth on that day, we don't know that he was actually born on Dec. 25th, and nothing in the Bible says he was. This birthdate for Jesus was decided on hundreds of years later. Also, I have never found anything that says Attis was born on Dec. 25th, other than this claim.

What about Attis' virgin birth? Well, it's hard to find anything like that in the story of Attis. It seems that one day Zeus (or Jupiter, as the Romans called him) saw Mt. Agdus, and it looked liked the goddess Rhea. (Don't ask me how a mountain looked like a goddess. Maybe Zeus was having trouble getting dates.) This got him so excited that he dropped some of his sperm on the ground, and from this came a creature named Agdistis. Agdistis turned out to be a really obnoxious guy, and the gods didn't like him, so one of the other gods, Dionysus, put wine in Agdistis' water to put him to sleep. Then, while Agdistis was asleep, Dionysus tied the end of a rope around Agdistis' genitals, tied the other end of the rope to a tree, yelled "Boo!" and – well, you can take it from there.

Agdistis bled all over the place thanks to this, and from that blood, a fruit tree sprang up, and much later, a girl named Nana happened by, picked some of the fruit, and put it in her lap. Then it disappeared. After this, she found herself pregnant with Attis.

Virgin birth? That doesn't sound quite right to me.

He was considered the savior who was slain for the salvation of mankind.

If we could sing a song about this one, it would start, "My baloney has a first name, it's A-T-T-I-S...."

Scholars who study the religion that started around Attis say that there's no evidence his religion even *offered* salvation or that Attis ever acted as a "savior". So obviously there's nothing for Christians to have copied.

He did die – we'll talk about that in a minute – but not because *someone else* did it. So he wasn't "slain" either.

His body as bread was eaten by his worshippers.

This is not known to be true. Worshippers of Attis, like worshippers of many pagan gods, had some sort of meal, but we do not know what it consisted of or whether it involved some sort of symbolism where the bread was thought to be his body.

On "Black Friday," he was crucified on a tree, from which his holy blood ran down to redeem the earth.

I have never found any truth in any of this. In the most famous story about him, Attis died *under* a tree, not crucified on it. There is no reference to it happening on a Friday, much less a "Black" one. Attis did shed blood, but all it did was make flowers (especially violets) grow, in some stories — if you want to call that "redeeming" the earth, then maybe your local farmer is doing the same thing by planting potatoes. It sure didn't "redeem" anything or anyone from sin (as Jesus did) or do those of us outside the florists' business a lot of good.

After three days, Attis was resurrected on March 25th (as tradition held of Jesus) as the "Most High God."

Is this true? I'm not sure. Which story do the people who claim this have in mind?

In one story, Attis is getting married, when Agdistis (remember him?) shows up at the wedding. Thanks to his interference, the bride dies. Attis then gets upset, falls under a tree, and then castrates himself, and then dies. Agdistis, seeing this, feels bad about it and asks Zeus to bring Attis back to life. Zeus is in a playful mood, so he says okay, but only a little: Attis' body doesn't rot, his hair continues to grow, and his little finger moves all the time.

Didn't like that one? Try this instead: A girl named Cybele falls in love with Attis, who prefers a nymph. Cybele kills the nymph. Attis goes crazy and castrates himself. From his blood, flowers grow out of the ground, and he turns into a pine tree.

Still not a happy enough ending? Okay, try #3: Cybele, who unknown to herself is the daughter of a king, marries Attis. When the king finds out about this, he kills Attis and makes sure the body is never found.

Do you see a resurrection here? You won't — that won't come for Attis until later, *after* Christianity gets going. And what about that date of March 25th? That was a festival called the Hilaria, and we don't find any proof that it was around any earlier than the 3rd or 4th century *AD* – several hundred years after Jesus.

Dionysus, the God Who Liked Wine

Even if you haven't heard of Attis, you've probably heard of Dionysus, or Bacchus as the Romans called him. He's another god that some say Christians stole from to create Jesus. Let's look at another list of claims.

Dionysus was born of a virgin on December 25th and, as the Holy Child, was placed in a manger.

Yes, it seems like every god was born on Dec. 25th, doesn't it? It must have been hard luck on the people who scheduled the parties.

We already pointed out that there's nothing to the Dec. 25th idea in the first place where Jesus is concerned, but more than that, just like Attis, I can't find any evidence from serious writers who do their research that it was when Dionysus was born, either.

As for being born of a virgin, Dionysus comes close to that – the same way Attis does. Although it depends which of the stories you want to believe. In the most popular story, Dionysus' mother was named Semele, and she was made pregnant by Zeus when he took the form of a lightning bolt. Later, Zeus' wife, Hera, tricked Semele into asking Zeus to reveal his glory, which ended up burning Semele to a crisp, leaving the unborn Dionysus behind. Zeus picked up the child and sewed him into his thigh until he was ready to be on his own.

Another story has Dionysus as the son of Zeus and Persephone. Yet another version has Dionysus "self-born". But there's nothing like a "virgin" conception or birth.

He was a traveling teacher who performed miracles.

First of all, as we said at the beginning: Any divine being (real or imagined) would be expected to teach or perform miracles, so this claim doesn't mean much. But in the case of Dionysus, the claim isn't very good anyway. In an ancient work of literature about Dionysus called the *Bacchae,* Dionysus does travel around Greece, Persia and Arabia spreading his rituals and delivering miraculous judgments on those who defy him. There are other stories in which he traveled around trying to make people more civilized, and one scholar has said that he was god who spent the most time traveling. This is not the same as Jesus traveling a limited area providing moral teachings, but there's a much closer alignment between Jesus and other Jewish "holy men" of his day (people like Honi the Circle-Drawer and Hanina ben dosa) who went around teaching and performing miracles.

Put it this way. If you come home and find a pizza box from a certain chain store in your trash, are you going to assume that someone bought that pizza from the chain store down the road, or the one in another state? And are you also going to say that the chain store near you stole the idea for using a box from another chain? No, because just as a box is exactly the sort of thing anyone would put a pizza in to keep in warm and safe, we'd also expect a prophet or divine person to teach and do miracles. That's their job. And if there were people doing stuff a lot like Jesus in his own neighborhood, then there's no need to say some god in another country far away and in a different culture was the inspiration.

He was a sacred king killed and eaten in a eucharistic ritual for fecundity and purification.

That's kind of hard to find. According to a story reported by Diodorus, an ancient historian, Dionysus as *an infant* was set upon Zeus' throne (a sacred king?) to play at being Master of the Universe. As he sat there, some of the Titans — bad boys of Greek mythology — snuck up with some toys and distracted him. While he was distracted, the Titans picked him up, tore him to pieces (killed), and boiled and roasted everything but his heart and ate it (eaten — in a eucharistic ritual?!?). When Zeus got wind of this, he became ticked as he often did, and blew the Titans to smithereens.

When it comes to life on earth, though, we have no evidence that the body of Dionysus was ever "eaten" by his followers in a ritual like this.

Dionysus rose from the dead on March 25th.

I have found no evidence to support the "March 25th" claim. As far as rising from the dead, we have a story that Dionysus was chased and persecuted by an enemy and descended to the depths of the Alcyonian

Sea, and to the land of the dead. We also have a story in which after the infant Dionysus was killed, his heart was used to make a new body. Nothing in any of these has more than a surface resemblance to what happened to Jesus. If we can equate "rose from the dead" so easily with both what happened to Dionysus and to Jesus, then you can also find a parallel to this in the haunted house ride at Disney World.

He was the God of the Vine, and turned water into wine.

It is true that Dionysus was the god of the vine, but the story of him turning water into wine comes from a time after the New Testament was written. There is also a story of how a fountain in a temple of Dionysus sometimes flowed with wine instead of water, but that was not water *turning into* wine.

Mithra, the God Who Didn't Put Up With Any Bull

The last god we'll look at is the one I get the most questions about – his name is Mithra. Mithra had a really interesting history. In his most ancient life, Mithra was the guy who went around dishing out punishment to people who broke treaties, and was responsible for bringing rain, vegetation and health. But later on, when the people in the Roman Empire found him, all of this changed and Mithra became mainly known for killing a "cosmic bull" which represented the constellation Taurus. Here's one last partial list of claims:

Mithra was born of a virgin on December 25th in a cave, and his birth was attended by shepherds.

If there was any god who was **not** born of December 25th, they'd probably change his birth certificate. Once again, the answer is the same: It's beside the point because Jesus is never said to be born that date in the New Testament.

So what about the rest? First of all, Mithra was *not* born of a virgin in a cave; he was born *out of solid rock.* I suppose technically the rock he was born out of could have been said to be a virgin! The part about the shepherds *is* entirely true, but the evidence for it dates at least *a century after* the time of the New Testament.

He had 12 companions or disciples.

This is false. This claim is based on a mistake in reading a picture of Mithra's bull-slaying framed by 2 vertical rows with 6 pictures each that are supposed to be signs of the zodiac, not "companions" or "disciples."

Mithra was buried in a tomb and after three days rose again. His resurrection was celebrated every year.

This is completely false. As one scholar who has studied Mithra a whole lot says, there is "no death of Mithras" — and so, of course, no rising again and no "resurrection" to celebrate.

His religion had a eucharist or "Lord's Supper," at which Mithra said, "He who shall not eat of my body nor drink of my blood so that he may be one with me and I with him, shall not be saved."

This one is *way* off base! The saying quoted is from a text written hundreds of years after Jesus lived, and the speaker is not Mithras, but Zarathustra. The closest thing that Mithraism had to a "Last Supper" was the eating of things like bread, water, wine and meat by the Mithraic believers, which was maybe a celebration of the meal that Mithra had with the sun deity after slaying the bull. But this sort of meal, as we said before, was the kind that was practiced by groups all over the Roman world — from religious groups to funeral societies.

1 Cor. 10:4 is "identical words to those found in the Mithraic scriptures, except that the name Mithra is used instead of Christ."

If anyone claims this is true, they need to get out those Mithraic scriptures and turn them over to Mithraic scholars at once, because they will want to know about them. Today's leading scholar of Mithraism, David Ulansey, says that "the teachings of the (Mithraic) cult were, as far as we know, never written down" and we "have been left with practically no literary evidence relating to the cult which would help (us) reconstruct its esoteric doctrines." (Maybe they found some Mithraic scriptures on eBay?)

So we've had a quick look at three gods – Attis, Dionysus, and Mithra – that some people claim, Christians were "copycats" with when they created

Jesus out of their imaginations. All three turned out to be bogus. There's a lot longer lists out there of other gods that the same kind of claim is made about, and you can learn more about those at the Internet addresses below. But before we finish with that, we have one more, "Hey, wait a minute…"

Justin Martyr: The Christian Who Let the Cat Out of the Bag?

Some people who use these "Copycat Jesus" theories like to point to some quotes from a guy named Justin Martyr, who was an early Christian writer from around 150 A.D:

> For when they say that Dionysus arose again and ascended to heaven, is it not evidence the devil has **imitated the prophecy**?"
>
> When we say that Jesus Christ was produced without sexual union, was crucified and died, and rose again, and ascended to heaven, **we propound nothing new or different** from what you believe regarding those whom you call the sons of Jupiter."

"See?" these say. "Justin is admitting that Christians stole stuff from the pagans!" Not so fast. Read the first quote carefully. Justin is saying that the devil has "imitated the **prophecy**". What he really is saying is that the devil looked at prophecies in *the Old Testament* and inspired Greek myths that he thought would imitate them.

Now look at the second quote. Justin writes this way not because he is admitting that Christians copied pagan stuff, but because the pagans themselves thought Christianity was *teaching new and different things*. Then he goes on to argue that when the devil "imitated" the prophecies of the Old Testament, the devil didn't get them right, as he goes on to say:

> And these things were said both among the Greeks and among all nations where they [demons] heard the prophets foretelling that Christ would specially be believed in; but that **in hearing what was said by the prophets they did not accurately understand it**, but imitated what was said of our Christ, **like men who are in error**, we will make plain.

So Justin isn't admitting anything about Christianity stealing ideas from pagans. Instead, he is trying to convince pagans (who disagree!) that there are parallels between the Greek myths and the *Old Testament*.

Read More!

<http://www.christian-thinktank.com/copycat.html>
<http://www.tektonics.org/copycat/copycathub.html>

The second one gives a huge list of alleged "copycat" gods, as well as more stuff on Mithra, Attis, and Dionysus.

Some of the people we have answers to, that you may encounter:

- Acharya S
- Kenneth Humphreys
- Timothy Freke and Peter Gandy
- Tom Harpur
- The "Zeitgeist" movie

Chapter 35:

I Dream of Genealogy

Matthew 1:1-17 and Luke 3:23-38 both offer a genealogy (list of ancestors) for Jesus. But they're way different from each other. Problem?

Some say no, because they suppose that the genealogy in Matthew belongs to Joseph's family, and the one in Luke applies to Mary, with Mary having picked up Joseph's legal ancestry through the Jewish custom called levirate marriage. This is how many church writers and scholars have answered the question.

But there is another idea that works just as well. In the ancient world, genealogies served a specific purpose, and it wasn't always to show who your ancestors were. Sometimes genealogies could serve another purpose. Matthew could, for example, by trying to demonstrate an *ideological* line listing people who God had blessed in Jewish history apart from the law. We can't be fully certain which, if either, of these answers is correct, but there are enough possibilities to say that there are good reasons why both Matthew and Luke can be reporting correct genealogies.

Read More!

<http://www.christian-thinktank.com/fabprof4.html>
<http://www.tektonics.org/gk/jesgen.html>

Chapter 36:

“I’m God. Okay?”

As Christians, we believe that Jesus was God in the flesh. Part of the reason we believe this is because we believe he claimed to be God.

But some people, though they may agree that Jesus said all the things the New Testament says he did, claim that what Jesus said didn’t mean he claimed to be God. So let’s look at what Jesus said about himself and see who’s right.

Wisdom. In our chapter on the Trinity coming up, we’ll talk about a figure in the Old Testament and in other Jewish books called *Wisdom.* Wisdom was an attribute of God, and so, it was part of God.

Jesus made several claims and did several things that show that he thought of himself as being Wisdom. In Proverbs, Wisdom invites people to come to eat dinner so that they can learn. Jesus dined with sinners and tax collectors because he was acting the part of Wisdom. In Matthew 12:42//Luke 11:31,

Jesus said he was "greater than Solomon," the wisest king of Israel, and this makes the most sense if he saw himself as Wisdom. In Matthew 23:34//Luke 11:49, which are parallels, Matthew's version has Jesus saying, "I will send them prophets..." while Luke's version has Wisdom sending the prophets.

Son of Man. This title comes from Daniel 7, where "one like a son of man" sits on a divine throne. The phrase used in Daniel for "son of man" is *bar enash.* In other languages of the time, this phrase meant an *heir or successor to royalty.* In Daniel, the one like a son of man is given rulership of the sort that God possesses, so the title, as used by Jesus, is his way of saying that he is *rightful heir* and successor to the throne of God.

It is also important that at his trial, Jesus said that he, as the Son of Man, will be *seated* at the *right hand* of God. It was audacious enough for Jesus to say he would be seated next to God (because you were supposed to stand in the presence of those above you), but that he also said he'd sit at God's right hand meant that Jesus would share the highest honors with God.

I AM. In John's Gospel (but also in Matthew 14:27), Jesus uses the phrase "I AM" to refer to himself. Although some think this is connected to God calling himself "I AM" in Exodus, most of the statements Jesus makes that use this phrase in a special way find parallels in the book of Isaiah where statements are made that only God can make.

Other claims. In Matthew 9:2 (and parallels in Mark 2:5, Luke 5:20 and 7:48) Jesus tells people that "their sins are forgiven." This may not seem significant, so an illustration is needed. If John does something bad to Joe, then Joe can forgive John. But it would be ridiculous for Jake - unless he were somehow related to Joe - to forgive John for what he did to Joe. Forgiveness requires the right to forgive. Therefore, Jesus' forgiving the sins of others that He had no personal connection with indicates that He believed that He was the only One who was offended by all sins and therefore had the right to forgive them: God, the author of all moral law.

In Matthew 8:21-2, with a parallel in Luke 9:59, it says, "Another disciple said to him, 'Lord, first let me go and bury my father.' But Jesus told him, 'Follow me, and let the dead bury their own dead.'" This doesn't seem to say much about Jesus' divinity, but it has to be considered with Leviticus 21:10-12. There, it is said that a high priest can never touch a dead body – not even one of his parents' bodies. This would mean that Jesus was claiming the very priority of the God who dwelt in the Holy of Holies!

These are just some of the most clear claims Jesus made to be God. There are others, but these are the hardest to dispute the meaning of.

One last thing – some critics make a big deal over that Jesus told people not to tell other people that he was Messiah, or that he healed them. This is sometimes taken to mean that Jesus really didn't believe he was God or Messiah, or had doubts. But this isn't what's happening. What's happening is that Jesus is watching out for people resenting him for claiming so much about himself, or acting like he was someone important. Remember what we said in an earlier chapter about honor. In this kind of society, saying or doing things that made you seem like you were better than other people was guaranteed to make people angry (even if you were being honest). So, Jesus had to extra careful about what he said and did, and had to tell people to keep quiet about him.

Read More!

<http://www.tektonics.org/jesusclaims/jesus-
claimshub.html>
<http://www.tektonics.org/qt/secretmess.html>

Chapter 37:

Jesus the Hypocrite

Christians believe that Jesus lived a sinless life, so naturally, critics will be interested in any proof they can get that Jesus committed a sin. (It's tempting to take it as an easy road, since they need to find only one sin!) Here's a few places where they think Jesus did something wrong.

#1: Jesus said not to get angry, but he got angry lots of times – like at people in the synagogue (Mark 3:5) and in the Temple. The first part misses out: What Jesus said was, "Anyone who is angry with *his brother* will be subject to judgment" (Matthew 5:22). None of the examples ever shows Jesus to be angry with his **brother** – which means, members of his group (such as disciples or apostles). He was exasperated with them sometimes, but not angry!

#2: Jesus was rude to his parents. What about "honor your father and mother"? There are two places this is said to happen. One is in Luke 2:49, where Jesus, when he was twelve, said to Mary and Joseph, "Why were you searching for me? Didn't you know I had to be in my Father's house?" For this one, though, you have to read "rudeness" into what Jesus is saying. Tone of voice says a lot, and we don't have any indication that Jesus was speaking rudely. (And actually, back in Jesus' day, it was considered right for a boy of this age to start being more independent like this; otherwise they'd become what was thought of as a "momma's boy.")

The other example often used is John 2:4, where Jesus says to Mary after she asks him to help miraculously make wine, "Dear woman, why do you involve me?" Some say the NIV covers up rudeness, but it doesn't. The word Jesus uses is the same word he uses all the time to address women in public, and it is also commonly used in Greek literature, and is used by a man in the history of the Jewish historian Josephus to call his beloved wife. The other half of the reply means literally, "What to me and to you?" and basically means, "This isn't any of our business." It *can* be impolite, but not always (compare 2 Kings 3:13 and Hosea 14:8).

#3: Jesus lied to his brothers. Critics will point to John 7:8, where Jesus says, "You go to the Feast. I am not yet going up to this Feast, because for me the right time has not yet come." They then point out that in John 7:10, he goes to the Feast anyway; and they add that "yet" shouldn't be in the text, because it is not in the original Greek. This last part is true, but there's still an answer that has to do with the culture Jesus lived in. To sum it up, it's kind of like the old moral story where you're asked, "If you're living in Nazi Germany and you're hiding Jews in your cellar, and the Nazis knock on your door and ask if you are hiding Jews, do you say yes or no?" You have a choice: Lie and preserve life, or tell the truth and get innocent people killed. Which do you do?

Most people will say at once that you lie, and that lying in that case is good. The same situation applies here, although the matter is not someone being killed. In this case, the problem is that Jesus' brothers do not believe in him, and are mocking him, so if they know he is going to the Feast, they will probably mock him there too and turn people away from him and the message of salvation. So as with lying to the Nazis, this was one of those cases where it was better to throw them off the trail.

#4: Jesus says to hate people (Luke 14:26). Not quite. There's another culture lesson here. As we said in another chapter, people in Jesus' time spoke in absolutes so that they could emphasize what they were saying. Someone could use the word "hate" to mean "love less."

Read More!

<http://www.tektonics.org/uz/yosef01.html>
<http://www.tektonics.org/lp/morgand01.html>
<http://www.tektonics.org/gk/jesussayshate.html>

Chapter 38:

Sign Your Gospel

Many people claim that the New Testament Gospels (as well as other parts of the Bible) are actually anonymous. They say we can't know who actually wrote them, and that the names of the authors that we have – Matthew, Mark, Luke and John – are at best, guesses made by people who edited the Gospels later, or at worst, just plain lies.

But people who say this sort of thing, I've noticed, are missing something important: They *never* explain how we can decide who wrote an ancient document – and they never compare the evidence of the Gospels to that of other ancient documents, whose authenticity and authorship is never (or is no longer) questioned.

Let's look at an example and make some comparisons. One of the most reliable works of ancient history is the *Annals* of Tacitus. No one disputes that

Tacitus wrote the *Annals*. Every single scholar agrees that he did. But how do we know this for sure?

Some people point out that the Gospel authors nowhere name themselves in their texts. But that's not entirely true. The Gospel authors **do** name themselves in the titles of their Gospels: "The Gospel according to...." And the same also happens to be true of the *Annals:* Tacitus never names himself in the *Annals*. His name is only found in the title. If someone wants to dispute this, then they need to provide some negative evidence, such as an ancient copy of Matthew without Matthew's name on the first page.

What about other types of evidence? We have the writings of many early Christians, from between 80-200 years of the time of Jesus, that tell us that the Gospels were written by the people whose names are on them. Compared to the *Annals,* we have a lot of this kind of information. In fact, we have no record of *anyone* saying that Tacitus was the author of the *Annals* for hundreds of years after they were written. The same thing can be said of numerous other ancient works.

There are many other clues that can tell us who wrote an ancient document. Let's look at those, using Tacitus as an example, and also looking at some examples that are sometimes used against the Gospels.

Anachronisms. Tacitus, supposedly, lived and wrote in the first and second century. So if his *Annals* contains a sentence that says that the Emperor Nero opened a *refrigerator*, took out a *burrito*, and stuck it in the *microwave oven*, we would have a good reason to doubt that the *Annals* (or at least part of them) were written in the first or second century – because obviously, things like microwaves didn't exist until the 20th century. (They did have burritos, but no one ever ate them because there was nothing to cook them with.)

An example of this type of argument used against the Gospels has to do with Matthew 27:8 and 28:15, which refer to things happening in Jesus' time that are still as they are "to this day." Critics say this means Matthew's Gospel was written very late, much later than Matthew was alive, and so he could not have written his Gospel. But how long can we wait before saying "to this day"? It doesn't take 40 years to have to say "to this day". The Berlin Wall fell in 1989, only 19 years ago. Why can't we say that it remains down "to this day"? So there is no reason why Matthew could not use "to this day" within his own lifetime.

On the other hand, we would also expect that Tacitus, in writing the *Annals,* would sound like the sort of person he was supposed to have been. Tacitus was an upper-crust Roman politician. We would expect him to have a high level of education, decent grammar, and a sophisticated tone suitable to the Roman upper-crust. He would not have a work full of spelling errors and mistakes. He would get governmental terms right (but maybe not, say, farming terms); he would probably also have a bad attitude towards people lower than he was (because upper class Roman people looked down on people lower than they were).

In the case of Matthew, we would expect someone who writes like he was a tax collector. Since being a tax collector wasn't popular, it was the sort of job most people took when they had no other choice. The evidence would suggest that Matthew had been trained as a priest or a rabbi, but couldn't find a job as one, and so became a tax collector. His Gospel shows that he had had religious training: He uses a lot of Old Testament quotes, and he also shows that he knows how to interpret Scripture the way the rabbis did. He also shows through his writing that he is an educated, cultured Jewish person: he has good Greek style, and would appear to be "at home" in the Roman world. This fits right in with the idea of Matthew the tax collector as author, because as a tax collector, he would have to serve the Romans and also become fluent in Greek.

So to put it in a nutshell, when we apply fair standards to the New Testament, it's impossible to doubt that every piece of it that has someone's name on it (meaning except Hebrews, which is anonymous) has the *correct* name on it.

Read More!

<http://www.tektonics.org/ntdocdef/gospdefhub.html>

Chapter 39:

The Three L's

Back in the 1940s a Christian named C. S. Lewis made an argument that is sometimes called, "Liar, Luantic, or Lord"? Lewis said that Jesus could only have been telling the truth about being the Lord, because "Liar" and "Lunatic" didn't make sense to describe him: He was too good of a person to be a liar; and he was too smart of a person to be a lunatic. Some people call this the "trilemma" argument.

Now this argument is still a good one, but that doesn't mean you should just use it by itself. For example, it won't work unless you have an argument showing that Jesus really said all the things that the New Testament says he did. Or if someone claims that Jesus was a space alien, then "the three L's" have to wait until you can try to get them out of *that* argument (good luck!).

But the logic of the argument is still good – because it breaks down to some very simple points:

Either Jesus claimed to be divine, or he did not. If He did not, words were put in his mouth by someone else. We talk a little about this in other chapters. But if Jesus did make those claims, then:

Either Jesus was right about those claims, or he was wrong. If He was right, Christianity is true. If he was wrong, then –

He either knew he was wrong, or did not know He was wrong. The first is the "liar" option of the trilemma. As for the second:

If he did not know he was wrong, he lacked knowledge because of an error in judgment. Errors in judgment have only two sources: A properly working mind, or an improperly working mind. The second is the "lunatic" option. The first is the "honestly mistaken" option, the most common attempt to add to the trilemma, though in a way it is really a form of the "liar" argument because it assumes a lie was told by Jesus about himself, without knowing it was a lie. But let's talk about this as through there were *really four options.*

Jesus the Liar?

This idea suggests that Jesus may have felt that his teachings were so important that it was worth him telling a lie about himself (saying he was deity) so that people would accept his teachings.

But there are many problems with this explanation. The first is that, other than his claims to divinity, Jesus' teachings were not so radical that they needed him to pretend to be divine to spread them. He could have simply claimed to be a specially inspired teacher, like one of the great rabbis. If anything, claiming to be divine would have put people off of his teachings, because he was claiming a special honor for himself, and that was the sort of thing that made people in that time suspicious and jealous.

Second, If Jesus were only a man and claimed to be God, was he an atheist himself? Did He think that the God of the Old Testament - who said, for example, "I will not give my glory to another or my praise to idols," (Is 42:8) and "I will not yield my glory to another," (Is. 48:11) - would not judge Him according to these standards? To have lied about being God, Jesus would have had to have had no fear of God whatsoever. He must have had some assurance that God wasn't going to incinerate Him for claiming to be divine and accepting the worship of others. To not fear God, Jesus would have had to have been an atheist - or else have had it "in" with the Father, which is precisely what Christianity claims of Him.

Put it another way: By Jewish understanding, to have accepted someone as the divine who was not would have been idolatry. To claim that you were divine when you were not would therefore have been unspeakably evil! As proof of this fact, we only need recall that the Jewish reaction to claims by the Roman Emperor to deity was quite extreme - so much so that the mighty Romans granted the Jews an exception to the requirement to accept the Emperor as a god.

"Whoops! I Thought I Was God..." - Jesus, the Honestly Mistaken?

How about this "fourth" option – that Jesus was simply honestly mistaken about being who He was?

I don't think so, and let me explain why. If someone thinks they are Superman, then they'll try to do things Superman does – like fly in the air, or bend metal in their bare hands, or see through walls. If they try and fail at these things, how long can they be "honestly mistaken" that they are Superman? Not long – and that's even more obvious when it comes to claiming to be God.

Jesus, the Candidate for Psychiatric Medication?

This option is one that is the most promising for critics, because we know of people with psychological or psychiatric disorders who claim to be God or Christ. It is also the argument that was used by some of Jesus' opponents (John 10:19-21).

The most serious problem with this argument is that nothing recorded about Jesus otherwise shows that he was mentally ill. If you ever want to see how people with this kind of disorder act, a good book (though very old) is Milton Rokeach's *The Three Christs of Ypsilanti*. Rokeach described three different people who thought they were Jesus Christ, and they all had very strange teachings and always wanted to be the center of attention. That doesn't fit Jesus.

Of course, critics might just say that Jesus really was crazy, and it wasn't recorded that he did stuff like put on tinfoil hats all the time. But any critic who says that sort of thing admits that the evidence we do have is against his argument.

Read More!

<http://www.tektonics.org/jesusclaims/trilemma.html>

Chapter 40:

Canon Fire

There's a lot of crazy stuff being said about how the books of the New Testament were picked. Some say that all the books people had in mind were thrown on a table, and if a book fell off the table, it wasn't put in the canon (collection of books in the New Testament). Others say the Roman Emperor Constantine forced people to accept the books he liked best.

None of this is true, except that maybe Constantine had an indirect influence on the canon long after the books were picked. And who picked them? The answer is, no one – in particular. The books were picked by the church as a whole.

Based on the writings we have from early Christians, here's what happened. There are 27 books in the New Testament. Of these, 20 were always and everywhere agreed to be authoritative. The other 7 books – 2 Peter, Jude, James, Hebrews, 2 and 3 John, and Revelation – were debated for a while because some people were not sure they were really written by the people whose names were on them. But eventually, they won out and were included.

What about books that were left out? We'll talk about those in the next chapter. We'll close *this* chapter by pointing out three things that were used to decide if a book belonged in the canon.

#1: The Rule of Faith

The "rule of faith" meant that nothing was accepted which included false doctrine. False doctrine was detected by looking at the history of what the church believed.

#2: Authorship

To make it into the canon, a work must have been authored by an Apostle or an immediate follower of an Apostle. This makes sense, because the persons most qualified to write about a great teacher or leader, whether it be Jesus, Martin Luther King, or Gandhi, are usually either: a) family (as with James and Jude), b) immediate followers (the Apostles), or c) immediate followers of those followers (Mark, Luke).

#3: Used by the Church

In other words, if the church had a history of using a book in its services, then that book had a chance to be in the canon. This means the church *at large* – some local churches liked certain books that were only known in their part of the world. These books never made it into the canon or were even considered for it.

So what about Constantine? Well, the most he did was wave his finger. Back when he took over the Roman Empire in the early 300s AD, he ordered that new copies be made of the New Testament, because pagan emperors before him had ordered so many copies destroyed. We're not even sure he knew what was in the New Testament when he made this order – he probably asked a church leader to oversee the project. Now once those copies were made, it'd be hard to argue that any books other that the ones in those copies belonged in the canon! Constantine may have helped the canon become more solid this way, but he didn't change it or mess with it – he left it to the experts in the church!

Read More!

<http://www.tektonics.org/lp/ntcanon.html>

Chapter 41:

Books With Their Pictures on Milk Cartons

There's also a lot of talk in the news every now and then about "lost" books that should be in the Bible. We could write a whole book (as some scholars have) about the different documents that people have claimed are authentic, but let's just talk about two that have been in the news recently – the "Gospel of Thomas" and the "Gospel of Judas".

The Gospel of Thomas, which claims to have been written by the Apostle Thomas (the one who is sometimes called "Doubting Thomas") is a list of sayings supposedly by Jesus. It's not like the Gospels in the Bible – it doesn't tell stories of healings or of the death and resurrection of Jesus. Most scholars think it was written by a group of people called Gnostics, who were heretics who believed that you got saved by learning their "secret" knowledge.

Let's start by asking why some people think Thomas should be thought of as an authentic book that was written very early, and may have some genuine information about Jesus.

"It's a list of sayings, just like another early Christian document, Q."

The first problem with this argument is that there's not even any evidence that Q existed (you can read about that in another chapter), and even if it did exist, we have no proof that it had nothing but sayings in it. But even if it did, lists of sayings or teachings existed long before Thomas (like the book of Proverbs) and also after Thomas (the Gospel of Philip, which no one thinks should be dated early) so there's no reason why this can prove that Thomas is early or authentic.

"Thomas has sayings just like some found in the New Testament Gospels, except that they look like they're more original than the versions in the New Testament."

Let's look at an example of this, from saying #89 in Thomas. This says: "Why do you wash the outside of the cup? Don't you understand that the one who made the inside is also the one who made the outside?" The New Testament versions of this verse are addressed to the Pharisees. Since the Pharisees are not mentioned in Thomas, some have said that Thomas 89 is an earlier tradition.

But does this make sense? There were no Pharisees in the second century, when most scholars think Thomas was written. So why would it not just be deleted? (Thomas does mention the Pharisees in two other places, but if the Pharisees were taken out of those sayings, they would lose *all* their context and meaning.)

"Thomas has sayings just like some found in the New Testament Gospels, except that they look like they're in a different order. The order they're in is more original than the versions in the New Testament."

The fact is that the things Jesus said must have been said in some order to start with. And if we can give a reason for Matthew, Mark, or Luke to have changed the order, then the same reasons could also be applied to the author of Thomas. So this argument can't go anywhere. However, we know from other documents that Gnostics like those that wrote

Thomas liked to change the order of things they took from other documents. We also know that the way Thomas is arranged is based on a system of "catch-words" (sort of like advertising slogans, but just one word!) in the Syriac language, which was not the language Jesus spoke.

On the other hand, what are some reasons to say that Thomas was written after the gospels now in the New Testament?

All the "hard" evidence says it came later.

If anyone wants to date Thomas early based on evidence, then it is fair to ask why the Gospels of the New Testament can't be dated early too, because they have much more evidence. As we saw in the chapter on the New Testament Gospels and who wrote them, and when, the New Testament Gospels are better off in the evidence department than many historical works. The same is true when it comes to documents like Thomas. If we dated Thomas on evidence of the earliest copy and the other factors we mentioned in our chapter on the Gospels, we'd have to put it in the second century.

Thomas promotes Gnosticism.

Gnosticism was a set of mystical beliefs from the ancient world that taught that you became saved by knowing certain secret facts. There were a lot of different ideas in Gnosticism, and it is clear that Thomas promotes some of them.

The reason this means Thomas must be dated later than the New Testament Gospels is because someone like Jesus, living in Jewish lands among Jewish people, could never have taught something like Gnosticism. Gnosticism was foreign to the thinking of Jewish people just as it was to Christians. If Jesus had been a Gnostic, the Sanhedrin would probably have laughed at him, not crucified him!

So there's no reason to think that the Gospel of Thomas has anything to say to us about the real Jesus. What about another "Gospel" that's been in the news lately, the Gospel of Judas? Well, it has the same problems that Thomas does. Hard evidence says it can't have been written earlier than the second century. And like Thomas, it is also Gnostic. In fact, the characters of Judas and Jesus sound more like something out of *Dragonball Z* than they sound like real people, as this sample shows:

> *"The twelve aeons of the twelve luminaries constitute their father, with six heavens for each aeon, so that there are seventy-two heavens for the seventy-two luminaries, and for each [of them five] firmaments, [for a total of] three hundred sixty [firmaments ...]. They were given authority and a [great] host of angels [without number], for glory and adoration, [and after that also] virgin spirits, for glory and [adoration] of all the aeons and the heavens and their firmaments.*

Documents like Thomas and Judas can be useful for understanding how later people misinterpreted and changed the teachings of Jesus. But when it comes to knowing what Jesus actually said, documents like Thomas and Judas would be more useful if you sold them on eBay.

Read More!

<http://www.tektonics.org/garagesale.html>
<http://www.tektonics.org/qt/thomasgospel.html>

Chapter 42:

Textual Trickery

How do we know that the New Testament says what its original writers originally put down – and that it wasn't changed over the years as it was copied?

Scholars use something called *textual criticism* to determine what a document said when it was first written. This can be applied to the Bible, although it is also applied to every other ancient or older work, whether it be a history written by the Roman author Tacitus or the plays of William Shakespeare.

When it comes to the New Testament, we have a lot of information – we have over 24,000 copies or parts of copies from ancient times, and they date from as early as 100 years after the New Testament was first written. (The earliest piece is a tiny scrap of the Gospel of John, with just a few words on it; and we have a few whole copies of the New Testament dating to the third century.) This is amazing considering that for many ancient works, all we have is less than a dozen copies which were made over a thousand years after the date the work was written.

Using textual criticism, we've been able to figure out what the original text of the New Testament said with 99% accuracy. To put that in perspective, that means that only a total of three pages in your average Bible give us any uncertainty. And all of that has to do with things that aren't that important.

But, you may ask, isn't this still a sign that people who copied the Bible may have been trying to change things, or may have messed up badly? Not at all. Nearly all of the mistakes made by people who copied the New Testament are easily to recognize as unintentional – things like spelling mistakes, or places where a change was made to make things clearer. For example, if a verse said, "He stood on the shore," and the "he" was clearly Peter (because it said so in other places), a scribe might change the "he" to "Peter."

Recently, however, a writer named Bart Ehrman has authored a book titled *Misquoting Jesus* in which he claims that *intentional* changes were made to many New Testament texts as a way of keeping heretics from reading the texts in a way that the church did not approve. There are a few places where Ehrman makes a good case for this. However, even in those cases it is hard to see any sort of serious problem, and in another book Ehrman even admits that scribes were trying to **preserve** the right meaning, not change it. For example:

> Luke 2:33 The child's father and mother marveled at what was said about him.

Some later copyists of the New Testament changed this verse to read, "Joseph and his mother marveled..." Why? Because there were heretics who were taking the original version above to mean that Joseph was Jesus' physical father, and so they denied the virgin birth. Of course, this was very silly anyway, because Luke clearly states that the conception of Jesus was the work of God (1:34-5), and Matthew elsewhere affirms the virgin birth. Besides, Joseph was certainly a "father" to Jesus in that important way of rearing him as a child, and we also would not expect Joseph to be referred to as, for example, "this man who acts as Jesus' father, but isn't".

Read More!

<http://www.tektonics.org/lp/nttextcrit.html>
<http://www.tektonics.org/books/ehrqurvw.html>

Chapter 43:

Oral Arguments

Have you ever played a game called "telephone"? You start with a room full of people, and one person whispers something in the ear of the next person, and what is said is passed around the room in whispers. By the time it gets to the other end of the room, it's completely different. You start with "four score and seven years ago" and by the time it is at the other side of the room, it becomes, "I have baloney in my slacks."

A lot of people use this game as an example of how the story of Jesus got distorted so that he became a figure of legend, who did miracles and rose from the dead, and said all kinds of things he never said. But there's a problem with comparing this to "telephone" – it doesn't match how people spread information in Jesus' day.

In the time of Jesus, 90% of the people could not read or write, so information was mostly transmitted by word of mouth. People of this time knew memory was not always perfect, just as we do, so they came up with ways to help people remember things – and what's interesting is that the techniques they used are much the same ones we use today to sharpen our memory. In fact, techniques used in today's "memory improvement" seminars, which some people pay a lot of money to attend, are some of the same techniques ancient people used.

Educated Jewish people used these techniques to memorize entire books of the Old Testament, if not the whole Old Testament. Ancient education consisted of memory exercises. Students were expected to remember the major events of narratives, although incidental details did not have to be remembered if the main point was not affected.

In addition, in a society that used oral transmission instead of writing, there could be a group of people that carefully guarded the oral transmission (like the Apostles) and made sure it was being transmitted accurately.

Instead of the game of "telephone" as described, imagine that the people in that room were made to repeat the sentence they were given over and over again until they got it right. Then imagine that someone listened in on every few people to check the message and correct any problems. That would be a better picture of what happened with the words and deeds of Jesus, according to what we know about the way ancient people transmitted important information. It wouldn't be as much fun of course – but it would be a lot more accurate!

Read More!

<http://www.tektonics.org/ntdocdef/orality01.html>
<http://www.christian-thinktank.com/loftus.html>

Chapter 44:

Q Tips

These days, when we watch a lot of TV, when we hear the letter "Q" used by itself, we may think of the mischievous and omnipotent character known by that name from *Star Trek: The Next Generation.* Or maybe we think of James Bond's gadget guru sidekick. But what does it mean when people refer to Q when it has to do with the Bible?

In a nutshell, Q is a document that was supposed to have been used, along with Mark, by Matthew and Luke when they wrote their Gospels. Supposedly

Matthew and Luke drew bits and pieces from both Mark and Q to write what they did.

Notice that I said "supposedly." I say this because no one has ever actually seen a copy of Q. No one knows all of what was in it, or even if it actually existed.

I also said that it is claimed that Matthew and Luke used Mark. This is called the theory of Marcan priority, because it says Mark wrote his Gospel first. Church history, though, says Matthew wrote his Gospel first (though maybe not in Greek as we have it).

It would take a long time to explain what it wrong with these ideas, but we can make a few points.

The first is that there is nothing necessarily wrong with saying Q existed or that Mark wrote first, if that is what the evidence shows us happened. But what happens is that some people go further and say that, for example, Q must have not had a lot of special stuff (like Jesus claiming to be God) that is important to Christians, and so it must have been written by people who were earlier than Christians, who did not believe Jesus was God. And then they say these people taught what truly happened, while Christians distorted what Jesus taught. Of course, even if it is correct that Q exists, and didn't say anything about Jesus claiming to be God, it would not mean it contained *everything* that the people who wrote it believed about Jesus. But the point is that this is more than just an idea of who copied who, but also *why* and what happened. And that's not valid when we don't even have a document in our hands.

Second, those who suggest this sort of copying often don't consider how it is that people in the first century exchanged information. They point to how Mark and Matthew seem so much alike, and suppose that there's no way this could have happened without one copying the other. But that's not necessarily true. Mostly in the first century, people exchanged information by speaking to each other, because as we said in the last chapter, around 90% of the people couldn't even read. And even when they could read and write, making copies was a difficult process. There was no such thing as a writing desk yet, and although tables were available, the idea to use them for writing had somehow not been thought of. A person who wanted to make a copy of something in the way the critics suggest had to assume an uncomfortable position on the floor (or perhaps a stool) as he wrote, and to copy from one scroll to another (scrolls had this nasty tendency to roll back up on you - sort of like books do not like to stay open to pages in the middle) would have had to engage in acrobatics that would make a circus manager proud.

The scroll written on had to be put on the floor (back breaking!) or on your knee or thigh, or sitting cross-legged as the scroll was stretched tightly from the point of one knee to the other. If Mark did copy Matthew directly (or vice versa), they would have done it by having someone else read the other work aloud while they took notes, and then used the notes to write everything from scratch otherwise, relying on memory to fill in everything they couldn't write down.

What this all means is that it's not a simple matter of just looking at how similar Matthew and Mark are, or Luke and Mark are, to decide who copied whom, or if anyone copied anyone at all. It also means something like Q isn't necessary. It is just as easy to say that Luke copied from Matthew at some point.

Some of the reasons given to say that Mark wrote first should also be looked at more closely. For example, one reason it is claimed Matthew copied from Mark is that Mark isn't a very good writer. It seems hard to believe, it is said, that Mark would "mess up" Matthew's much better writing. But because of the reasons we have above (transmission by speaking, taking notes) that just isn't hard to believe at all. People who rewrote stuff in the first century did it in their own style. We also know that later writers who copied Mark to write their own documents (like apocryphal gospels) "messed up" Mark and sounded less fancy than Mark did. So just because Mark's writing is not as good as Matthew's does not mean only Matthew could have copied Mark.

My view is that Matthew and Mark were both working from the same collection of oral stories told by all the Apostles, and that Luke used stories from Mark and from an earlier version of Matthew in Aramaic. But this is a big, complicated topic – if you want to look into it more, you'll have a lot of reading to do!

Read More!

<http://www.tektonics.org/qm/qmhub.html>

Chapter 45:

Harmonic Convergences

If you've ever read two Gospels at the same time, and compared them, you might have wondered about why they report the same events differently.

The answer to why can be different, depending on what story is being reported and what Gospels are being read. But overall, Christians would argue that the Gospels present complementary, not contradictory, accounts of what happened.

There are also certain points to consider about the way people in the time of the Bible wrote stories about history. They used certain techniques that we would find strange. When we look at reports of the same event from two different writers, we think they should report **exactly** the same thing. But an ancient writer sometimes thought that they should report things in *different* ways, for different reasons.

Here's an example. Compare Mark 5:1-10 with Matthew 8:28-31. They are obviously the same story, but Matthew has two demon-possessed men, while Mark has only one. Why?

Some people answer by saying there were two, and Mark just mentions one and not the other. That's okay as an answer. We can find the same sort of thing in secular histories.

But there's another answer I like better myself. Let me illustrate it with another example.

If you have a red-letter Bible (one with Jesus' words in red), look at Matthew closely. You'll notice that the teachings of Jesus form five major sections. This is something Matthew intentionally did – why we are not sure; maybe because he was trying to have five "blocks" of Jesus' teachings, like there were five books of Moses. But the point is that Matthew purposely arranged things a certain way, and that way was not necessarily in chronological order.

I think that what happened with the story of the demon-possessed men is that Matthew, like Mark, had two different stories about demon-possessed men (the other is found in Mark 1:23-36). But because he wanted to leave more room for teachings of Jesus, he took the demon-possessed man from the story recorded in Mark 1:23-26 and put him in the other story.

You may say that seems like a stretch. It isn't – not for the time Matthew was writing. We can find examples of the same sort of practice in secular histories of that time. Writers felt free to move things around for various reasons. The truth is that when we judge the Gospels by the standard of the day they were written, all the alleged problems disappear.

Read More!

<http://www.tektonics.org/harmonize/lincoln01.
html>
<http://www.christian-thinktank.com/ordorise.html>

Chapter 46:

The Secret Scroll Conspiracy!

What are the Dead Sea Scrolls? Do they contain things that are harmful to Christianity? There are writers who have claimed that this is the case, and have even suggested that the church is trying to hide or suppress the Dead Sea Scrolls. But this is all false.

The Dead Sea Scrolls contain two different types of documents. First, they contain copies of the Old Testament, and also some Jewish religious books that are not in the Bible. But not the New Testament.

Second, the Scrolls contain copies of documents that were special books for and about the people who wrote them. The owners of the Scrolls were called Essenes, and they had headquarters in caves near the Dead Sea in Israel. The Scrolls were part of a library they kept, and it included books about their rules for living, and how they interpreted the Old Testament.

Although some have gone so far as to claim that the Essenes were Christians, the facts do not bear this out. It is true that the Essenes had some things in common with Christians, but that is because both had a lot of Jewish heritage in their movements. But there were also many important differences:

1. The Essenes were very concerned with obeying the Law of the Old Testament, whereas in the New Testament, the Law, although treated with respect, is considered less important. For example, though Jesus allowed life-saving rescue on the Sabbath, the Essenes forbade it if any instrument was required to do it.
2. The Essenes expected worship at the Temple in Jerusalem to be cleaned up. Christians expected the Temple to be destroyed, to be

replaced by God and Jesus and a Jerusalem with no Temple.

3. Celibacy (not ever having sex) was required for most Essenes, but only a limited ideal for some in the Christian movement.
4. The Essenes would not engage in arguments with outsiders. Christianity was a missionary faith in constant conversation with outsiders.
5. Christianity welcomed sinners and the unrighteous to repent while the Essenes preferred to avoid sinners.
6. Christians baptized once and for all. Essenes had repeated baptisms.
7. The Essenes believed in two Messiahs, one priestly, the other political. In Christianity Jesus was seen as filling both offices.
8. Jesus rejected any idea that his followers will conduct a physical war to begin the Kingdom of God, while Essenes predicted such a war, with angels fighting on their side.

People who make these kinds of arguments that we have answers to:

- Michael Baigent

Read More!

<http://www.usc.edu/dept/LAS/wsrp/educational_site/dead_sea_scrolls/>

Chapter 47:

Make Believe Jesus

There are critics who say that the New Testament authors just "made up" stuff that they say about Jesus. One group called the Jesus Seminar claimed that nearly all of the things Jesus said and did in the Gospels were just made up by Christians who lived long after Jesus. Is this true?

There are a number of reasons to think that it is people like the Jesus Seminar who are making things up, rather than the New Testament.

1. **If these things were made up, why did the church create such a difficult faith to follow?** Certainly they could have made things much easier on themselves by, for example, permitting sacrifices to the Emperor of Rome. They also could have put words in Jesus' mouth about important issues such as circumcision and speaking in tongues. That Jesus does not address issues like these is

good evidence that the church didn't make things up for Jesus to say after he was gone.

2. **Some of the material critics understand as late, isn't.** For example, in Matthew 16:18 and 18:17, the word "church" is used. It is assumed that there was no "church" until after Jesus was gone. But the Greek word, *ekklesia*, was used to refer to official meetings of the people of Israel – in other words, any worship assembly, including the Jewish synagogue. So it isn't a reason to think the saying was made up for Jesus.
3. **Eyewitnesses would not permit such creation.** In the first Christian generation there would be eyewitnesses – friendly and hostile – who would exert control over the transmission of things Jesus said and did. The book of Acts shows that the church was a well-organized group that exchanged information and had a hierarchy of leaders who made sure that teachings were accurate and approved. Some critics claims that there were "prophets" in the early church who claimed to speak for the Risen Jesus, and that sayings offered by these "prophets" were transferred to the earthly Jesus. But there is no evidence that such prophets existed, and what little evidence we have in the New Testament shows that any revelation from the Risen Jesus is attributed to the Risen Jesus, like the book of Revelation.

Read More!

<http://www.tektonics.org/ntdocdef/gospdefhub.html>

Chapter 48:

Along the Bias

"Who can believe what the New Testament says? It was written by people who had a bias – something they were trying to 'sell' to other people."

Something like this is very easy to say, but it can't just be said to be relevant – it needs to be **argued** and proven or shown likely to be relevant. Just because someone is biased does not mean what they say is not true – in fact, you may as well say that they are biased *because* they are telling the truth. The truth itself is very heavily "biased" – because it is **true**!

What people often mean when they claim the Bible is "biased" is that they think the authors of the New Testament were so anxious to convince people that they stretched the truth or made things up. But does the New Testament show this?

The burden to show that it does is on those who make the accusation. Just as in our courts today, a person is "innocent until proven guilty," so it is up to the "prosecutor" – the doubter – to make their case. What would they need to do to do this?

First, they would need to show that an author was someone who was undiscerning or gullible, or showed that they couldn't tell fact from fiction. How could they do this?

One way is to claim that the reporting of miracles in the Bible proves this already about the Bible's authors, but that's only shifting the focus to another argument (as to whether miracles can happen) which needs to be argued separately.

Another way is to point to other religious people who are gullible (especially people who lived at different times and places!) and claim that this supports a claim that a Bible author was gullible. But that's guilt by association. If that can be argued, then we can use people like Josef Stalin to "prove" that all atheists are evil mass murderers.

Yet another way is to claim that different accounts of the same events contradict each other (like the Gospels). But that too is a separate argument. It has to be shown that the "contradictions" exist and are serious, more serious than they should be compared to other historical accounts that report the same events, as written by different authors (see the other chapter on this, "Harmonic Convergences"). Secular historians do not consider such contradictions important to saying something happened if they involve details rather than the main event (for example, if there was a contradiction over whether or not Jesus was crucified, this would be a problem; but not if there are slight variations in what Jesus said from the cross).

One last way is to point out that the New Testament itself says it is trying to prove something (such as when John says he wrote that a reader, "might believe that Jesus is the Christ, the Son of God" (John 20.31). But *all* history is written so that people will know (and believe) what is reported. And other ancient historians like Thucydides and Josephus use the same type of language.

In addition, someone who claims that the New Testament authors were so biased that they made things up needs to explain why so much of what is reported doesn't take the chance to make the authors and others look better. In the Gospels, the apostles often look slow to learn, foolish, or afraid, which is not what we would expect if they were "biased".

They must also explain the signs of eyewitness testimony in the reports: Things like incidental details that are reported which add nothing to the story, while it is also clear that they did not take chances open to them to make things seem greater than they were. For example, when Luke reports the healing of the son of the widow of Nain (Luke 7:11-16), the crowd calls Jesus a "great prophet" – if Luke was making things up to prove something, this would have been a perfect place for him to have the crowd say Jesus was Messiah, the Son of God, and so on. But he didn't. (That does not mean there might not be times when people *did* say this sort of thing, but the fact that it is missing, where someone "biased" as Luke is supposed to be, could have inserted it, suggests that he isn't making things up at all.)

Then they have to explain why the Gospels didn't put answers in Jesus' mouth about problems facing the church in Paul's day – things like the circumcision of Gentiles, or speaking in tongues.

Of course, someone could say that this was part of some trick – for example, that the disciples purposely made themselves look bad so they could fool people into thinking they were telling the truth! – but at that point, it is theory that drives the facts, not facts that dictate the theory.

Read More!

<http://www.christian-thinktank.com/nuhbias.html>

Chapter 49:

Fictional Friction

There are a bunch of arguments that have been made – by a few different people – that the New Testament is nothing but fiction based on "rewrites" of the Old Testament (or maybe the works of Homer, or something else). What critics who use this argument do is find some passage of the New Testament that looks like something from the Old Testament. They then claim that the New Testament author just read the Old Testament story, thought it was good, and made up some new story using the Old Testament story.

For example, one critic pointed out that there were similarities between descriptions of Elijah in 2 Kings 1, and of John the Baptist in Mark 1:6. Both are described as wearing a "leather belt" around their waists. From this, we are apparently to figure out that Mark just made up things about John in order to match him to Elijah. John, so it is argued, probably didn't wear a leather belt on his waist; Mark just made it up because he wanted people to think John was "another Elijah." (Maybe they also think John just let his pants fall down all the time, or wore a three piece suit and a tie.)

There's an obvious problem, though. If Mark can "make up" John's leather belt based on the description of Elijah, then why can't John have read 2 Kings 1 **himself** and come up with the same idea, because *he* (John) wanted people to think he was another Elijah?

Ancient people were more into "showing it" and "doing it" than we were. Jesus purposely chose 12 disciples to represent the 12 tribes of Israel, and stayed 40 days in the wilderness to purposefully parallel the Exodus. Similarly today, a hunger striker may fast exactly 14 hours, one for each of 14 prisoners being held against their will.

When we see parts of the New Testament that use words from, or seem a lot like, the Old Testament, it is more likely that either a) the character in the story, like Jesus, *purposely* did something that was like an Old Testament story, because he wanted people to see a similarity; 2) a New Testament writer saw or knew of an actual event in history, thought about whether it sounded like something from the Old Testament, and if it did, used their literary skills to compose a description of what actually happened, using Old Testament stories to draw words from to create the description.

The point is that whether something a text reports happened, did happen, should be determined by tests such as, "Is it plausible as history?" — not by whether it sounds like another story. There are all kinds of real, historical parallels between the assassinations of Abraham Lincoln and John F. Kennedy. A writer could look for key phrases that could be taken from a Lincoln biography and use them in a Kennedy biography. Here, for example, are some phrases from a book describing Lincoln's assassination: "gunshot rang out," "frozen instant," "enveloped in smoke," "slumped forward," "deranged, incomprehensible terror," "screams, a medley of voices." All of these could be used just as easily in an account of Kennedy's assassination.

There's another issue related to this one. In Matthew 2:15, Matthew quotes Hosea 11:1:"When Israel was a child, I loved him, and out of Egypt I called my son." He says that Jesus "fulfilled" this passage when he came out of Egypt. But if we look at Hosea, it is clear that he is talking about Israel coming out of Egypt, not Jesus. Is Matthew misusing Hosea?

This is something many critics claim of this and many other Old Testament passages used by the New Testament. But this is like claiming that a basketball player is breaking the rules of soccer when he passes the ball to another player with his hands. We need to understand that the rules were different then for how people could use the Old Testament to argue for something. And once we understand how that worked, it becomes clear that Matthew did **not** abuse the Old Testament.

Jewish religious scholars in and around the time of Jesus used several different forms of *exegesis* (interpreting Scripture). We don't need to talk about all of these, but the most important one to remember is a type called *midrash.*

Midrash was a way of reading the Old Testament that made it more relevant to people living at a later time. To do this, a teacher was allowed to take sentences, phrases, or even single words "out of context" and apply them to a new situation in his own day. This may seem strange to us, but for the Jewish teacher, it was a way of showing that God was still acting in history in the same (or similar) ways as He did in the Old Testament.

Once we understand this, it is not hard to see what Matthew was doing with Hosea. As he saw it, by coming out of Egypt, Jesus was *re-enacting* Israel's trip out of Egypt as reported by Hosea. When he says "fulfilled," he doesn't mean Hosea predicted Jesus would come out of Egypt. He means Jesus acted the same way as Israel did. (Think "fulfilled" in the same way you might say someone "fulfilled" a contract by doing what it said needed to be done.)

This is just one example of the New Testament using the same rules to interpret the Old Testament as the Jewish teachers of their day did. There were even several rules for how this could be done, and we can find many examples of the New Testament authors using these rules.

People we have answers to who use these kinds of ideas:

- Randel Helms
- Dennis MacDonald

Read More!

<http://www.tektonics.org/gk/helmsr01.html>
<http://www.tektonics.org/gk/homermark.html>
<http://www.tektonics.org/af/abehomer.html>
<http://www.christian-thinktank.com/baduseot.
html>

Chapter 50:

Slave Drivers, Part 2

We read the New Testament and see many references to slaves and slavery. Automatically, we might think there's something wrong here. Isn't slavery bad? Then why isn't the Bible condemning it?

Slavery in Roman times was something like the slavery we know from American history. There were some differences. In the Roman world, for example, a slave could become very important, even owning their own slaves. They even had certain rights as slaves. And slaves in the Roman world were set free much more often than slaves in America. But it was still a harsh system with a lot of problems.

So why doesn't the New Testament say more against it? In fact, why doesn't Jesus condemn slavery?

We would not expect Jesus to say anything about slavery, because where he was, in Judaea, the people he talked to were mostly poor people. They would not own slaves, so it would have been as pointless to talk to them about slavery as it would have been to talk to them about not smoking cigarettes. Even rich people in Judaea usually didn't own slaves. It just wasn't something the people Jesus spoke to did.

On the other hand, later New Testament writers say a lot about slavery, but it seems all wrong when we just glance at it and think of American slavery. Paul and Peter say things to slaves like, "obey your master." Some people think that they support slavery because of this.

But we have to read the Bible more closely to understand what is happening. Slavery is not being endorsed, but is actually being undermined, very subtly, by passages like the ones that tell slaves to obey their masters, and many others in the New Testament.

Do you know anything about Mahatma Gandhi? Or Martin Luther King? Both of these leaders advocated non-violent resistance as a way to reform society. They didn't head-on attack the people who oppressed them. Instead they used subtle tactics to eat away at the power people held over them. This is what the New Testament is like when it comes to slavery.

A head-on assault, like Paul demanding, "Free the slaves!" would have caused more problems than it solved. Slaves that were set free would have no means of support, and many would simply die. Since slaves were as much as 40 percent of the population of the Roman Empire, widespread, immediate freedom would have been a disaster causing the loss of countless lives. An immediate call for freedom would also have brought action from the Roman government. Rome dealt with slave revolts harshly and with brute force.

Like Gandhi and King, the New Testament "revolted" against slavery in a better way. Paul says in Galatians 3 that there is "neither slave nor free" in Christ. One of the ways slavery was kept alive was by viewing slaves as unequals. It would be hard to keep someone as a slave if you were told they were your equal, or if you did keep them, you would hardly be able to treat them like slaves.

You may say, "But Peter and Paul both advise slaves to be obedient." Slaves, however, were expected to be lazy and *dis*obedient. To undermine the expectation of their masters was a subtle but powerful way to subvert also the entire institution of slavery from the ground up. Also, slave masters were told to be fair and just (Col. 4:1). Once again this means that they had to view slaves as equals.

The New Testament doesn't approve of slavery. It does recognize it as something that exists, and that the greater political powers allowed to exist. The New Testament teaches that change should be instituted from "the inside outward" and should be a matter of individual moral decision. And as Gandhi and King both realized, that is the best way to make changes in the way people think over the long term.

Read More!

<http://www.christian-thinktank.com/qnoslavent.html>

Chapter 51:

Common Census, Part 2

Luke is usually thought of as a guy who got the details of history right – even by scholars who think he was wrong about Jesus rising from the dead. But there is one thing he wrote that's often said to be wrong, and we hear about it every Christmas: The story of how Augustus Caesar conducted a census, at the time of a lower ruler named Quirinius.

Some think Luke is confused with a census that took place later – about 10 years after Jesus was actually born. This is based in part on the fact that Quirinius ruled 10 years later than Jesus was born. (Jesus was born around 4 B. C. – not 0 B. C. – and Quirinius ruled around 6 A.D.)

There are a couple of ways to answer this. One idea is that Quirinius ruled two different times, and that Luke is referring to an earlier post he held. But the information on that is sketchy, so we can't be sure of it.

Another idea is that Luke's grammar means he's actually saying that what he records happened "before the census of Quirinius" (not "the first census of Quirinius"). This is possible but not certain.

A third idea is that Luke's census was connected to an event we know happened about the time Jesus was born: There was a registration in which people had to take an oath of loyalty to the Emperor. It also may have been a census related to property, not people, which would explain why Joseph had to go to Jerusalem, where, as a descendant of David, he may have owned land.

There are many questions raised about Luke's accuracy here, but as time has passed, scholars have come to recognize more and more that Luke got right.

Read more!

<http://www.tektonics.org/af/censuscheck.html>
<http://www.christian-thinktank.com/quirinius.html>

Chapter 52:

Doesn't Like Girls, Part 2

There are critics who think the New Testament, and Paul in particular, is "anti-woman." There are a few different passages that they appeal to in order to prove this, but let's take a close look at the two that are most commonly used.

The first is 1 Corinthians 14:33-36:

> For God is not a God of disorder but of peace. As in all the congregations of the saints, women should remain silent in the churches. They are not allowed to speak, but must be in submission, as the Law says. If they want to inquire about something, they should ask their own husbands at home; for it is disgraceful for a woman to speak in the church. Did the word of God originate with you? Or are you the only people it has reached?

This seems all too clear – Paul is saying to women, "Sit down and shut up!" But let's take a closer look.

First of all, the phrase, "as in all the congregations of the saints" should be a complete sentence with the previous sentence, "For God is not a God of disorder but of peace." The only other time Paul uses this phrase, it is for the end of an argument (1 Cor. 11:16), not the beginning.

Second, the evidence shows us that what Paul says in most of this passage is not his own words, but words of *opponents* that he is quoting back to the Corinthians, and then *refuting*. There are two lines of evidence that show this. For one, there's a tiny Greek word in the original (which shows up in the KJV as "What!" but doesn't show up in the NIV at all) which Paul in other places in his letters uses as a harsh reaction to a mistaken position he then refutes (for example, Romans 9:20-21). For another, if this passage means women have to be silent at *all* times, then Paul openly contradicts himself, because he has previously in this letter given instructions about women praying and prophesying.

The other most famous passage used to prove Paul hates women is 1 Timothy 2:11-14:

> A woman should learn in quietness and full submission. I do not permit a woman to teach or to have authority over a man; she must be silent. For Adam was formed first, then Eve. And Adam was not the one deceived; it was the woman who was deceived and became a sinner.

This one is a little more complicated. Critics think it means Paul is saying women should shut up and have babies, or else they won't be saved. But when we understand who he was talking to and why, it makes a lot more sense.

The command to learn in silence in verse 11 needs an important background qualifier: In the New Testament's time, men *and* women were both supposed to be quiet and submissive when they were being taught. It was just the way you were supposed to respect a teacher. "Don't talk in class" was the rule for both men and women. So what this means is that Paul is probably talking to people who thought women should be exempt from this rule. Why? We'll see in a minute.

The second issue is the word which we translate as "exercise authority over." This is the only place we find this word in the New Testament, and we are not sure what it means, but it seems to mean to *dominate* or to take authority away from someone else who rightly has authority.

The third issue is with the word "teach" and it is related to the second issue. The grammar of the verse tells us that "teach" is linked to "exercise authority over." In other words, one qualifies the other. So this is not a restriction on women teaching at any time, but on women teaching at the same time as they "exercise authority over" other people.

What this means is, Paul is correcting a situation in which women "exercise authority over" (in a domineering way) *and* teach men, at the same time. But what would cause this to happen? The clues are found in what else Paul goes on to say. Notice the points he goes on to make:

- Adam was created before Eve
- It was NOT Adam who was deceived, but Eve.
- Childbearing is important and good

Why would Paul say things like this? Probably because he was answering someone who was teaching that:

- Eve was created before Adam (or at the same time?)
- Adam was deceived; Eve was not.
- Childbearing is 'bad'

And what do you know? The place where Timothy was – the city of Ephesus – just happened to be one of the strongest *goddess worship centers* in history. It was also a place where we know there were people who "rewrote" Bible texts. It is just the kind of place where we'd expect someone to rewrite Genesis so that Eve came first and didn't make a mistake like Adam did. Ephesus was also a place where we could find some early versions of that mystical teaching called Gnosticism we talked about before – a teaching system which believed that women were the origin of men, and that Eve was enlightened, not deceived, by the serpent. (This may also mean that "exercise authority over" means, "claim that women were the origin of men".)

But then what about "saved through child-bearing"? That also looks a lot like an answer to a pro-woman Gnostic-type group. Some Gnostics believed that it was wrong to have children (and even didn't allow marriage) because it trapped a soul in a body. The people Paul was answering probably claimed that women would lose salvation if they bore children, so it was necessary for Paul to affirm the opposite.

Read More!

<http://www.christian-thinktank.com/fem09.html>

Chapter 53:

The Masked Apostle vs. Jesusbro!

Rom. 3:28 For we maintain that a man is justified by faith apart from observing the law.

James 2:24 You see that a person is justified by what he does and not by faith alone.

Some people think James and Paul directly contradict one another here. But they need to look more closely at what James and Paul are talking about. Just because two people use the same words doesn't mean they mean the same things by them (especially since, as we've said before, languages at this time had a lot fewer total words).

Paul says in Romans 3 is that "Therefore no one will be declared righteous in his sight by observing the law" (3:20) In other words, no one shall be justified by doing the law, because no one actually "does" the law! We **all** violate it at some point. Paul is speaking of a time *prior to* someone becoming a Christian. James 2:10 even agrees and ups the stakes: "For whosoever shall keep the whole law, and yet offend in one point, he is guilty of all." The two are in perfect agreement so far: The law does not save, because no one is able to perfectly fulfill it.

But now look at James 2:17, "…faith by itself, if it is not accompanied by action, is dead." That word "dead" says it all. Someone who does not do works clearly has no faith to speak of, none that is living. In other words, if you really and truly believe Jesus died for you, you'll act like he did! Paul in his letters is always telling people to be moral and do good things because they belong to Christ. This is said no better than it would be in James 1:22-24:

> Do not merely listen to the word, and so deceive yourselves. Do what it says. Anyone who listens to the word but does not do what it says is like a man who looks at his face in a mirror and, after looking at himself, goes

away and immediately forgets what he looks like.

But how can they *seem* to contradict then? It is because Paul and James are not even addressing the same issues. Paul is teaching that you can be justified and saved apart from *rituals* associated with observation of the Jewish law, such as circumcision (Rom. 3:1). James is talking about the practical outworking of belief or faith through generally moral behavior, but not through anything uniquely associated with the Jewish law. Is there any mention of circumcision or Jewish holidays in James? No — he is concerned with caring for the poor, treating all people fairly, and holding one's tongue in check, *once you are a believer*. As one writer put it, "The works of faith which James advocates are different from the works of the law that Paul condemns."

Let's explain it in more detail. The Old Testament law was no cold moral code; it was a written expression of God's moral law. Paul knew this (Romans 1-2) as did every other Jewish teacher before and since. The sticklers of Paul's time, however, had the idea that "if we just followed the law to the letter" they would please God through their strict adherence and the Old Testament promises of blessing would come true (the egghead term for this is "covenantal nomism"). So, to the Roman church, Paul emphasizes that the purpose of the code was to increase consciousness of sin (3:19-20) - as opposed to those who asserted that following the letter, to the point of circumcision (4:9-12), was what was the key to salvation. Paul points out, through his example of Abraham, that faith came first and was given credit, for after all, Abraham was counted as righteous before Moses saw the light of day. (4:9ff) So it cannot be following the bare moral code that leads to salvation.

In contrast, James says not a word about circumcision or following the written code. He speaks of application as a result of a living faith, after becoming a believer. Nor does he use Abraham's following of the "law" as proof of his righteousness: He points to his actions that proved his faith in God. Paul and James are answering different questions.

Read More!

<http://www.tektonics.org/gk/jamesvspaul.html>

Chapter 54:

The Masked Apostle vs the Fishwhacker

Galatians 2:11-14 When Peter came to Antioch, I opposed him to his face, because he was clearly in the wrong. Before certain men came from James, he used to eat with the Gentiles. But when they arrived, he began to draw back and separate himself from the Gentiles because he was afraid of those who belonged to the circumcision group. The other

> Jews joined him in his hypocrisy, so that by their hypocrisy even Barnabas was led astray. When I saw that they were not acting in line with the truth of the gospel, I said to Peter in front of them all, "You are a Jew, yet you live like a Gentile and not like a Jew. How is it, then, that you force Gentiles to follow Jewish customs?

A lot of people look at this passage and think this was the church's version of *Monday Night Raw*. Some think that behind this "fight" was also a big split between Christians on Paul's side who believed in salvation without works, and Christians on Peter's side who believed in salvation *with* works. Then they say that Paul's side won the fight, and that's why we believe what we do today.

Yeah, right.

The fact is that the real reason for this fight had nothing to do with works or salvation. It had to do with something we talked about in the chapter, "Reading Leviticus Can Be Fun" — *ritual purity*. In Paul and Peter's time, like in the Old Testament, people put things in different categories of "clean" and "unclean". This didn't have to do with dirt exactly, but with whether things or people were more or less like God than other things, or closer to what God wanted than other things.

Jewish people at the time of Jesus had a lot of rules about ritual purity, many of them derived from the Old Testament, but some added on top of it. One of these rules was that eating with Gentiles (non-

Jewish people) was a bad thing because Gentiles were "unclean".

Peter and Paul were both born Jewish, so all their lives they had become used to living by these rules. So had a lot of other early Christians who had been born Jewish. Jesus set a new standard because he didn't have any problem meeting with or touching people that were supposed to be "unclean". But sometimes old habits are hard to break. Let's look at these verses a little at a time now.

> When Peter came to Antioch, I opposed him to his face, because he was clearly in the wrong. Before certain men came from James, he used to eat with the Gentiles. But when they arrived, he began to draw back and separate himself from the Gentiles because he was afraid of those who belonged to the circumcision group.

We can see here that Peter is said to have *previously* eaten with Gentiles. What has now happened is maybe that "certain [men] from James" witnessed this "violation" where Peter sat with Gentiles, and either they did not approve or else he thought they did not approve. It's more likely that he just *thought* they didn't approve, because otherwise Paul would have said something about the men from James doing the wrong thing.

Again, Peter already *had been* associating with Gentiles in ways that were looked at as wrong according to the purity rules of Judaism. He had also been disrespected for it (Acts 10:24-11:18). But why would this happen? Weren't the other Christians aware of what Jesus had done? Sure, but there was an unusual problem. Peter had been picked to bring the Gospel to Jewish people. If these Jewish people who were not yet Christians saw Peter eating with Gentiles, they'd consider him "unclean" and not want to talk to him. So Peter had a kind of obligation to still follow the Jewish rules for keeping "clean." They also might think he was disrespecting Jewish people.

Ordinarily, then, what Peter was doing was what he was supposed to do. But this time, he sat away from Gentiles while he was in Antioch. He was not in danger of offending any of the Jewish people he was supposed to be a missionary to. Why he did this we can only guess. Maybe he was afraid of Jewish people who disliked Gentiles a whole lot trying to hurt him. (There was a Jewish group called the Zealots around this time who were kind of the terrorists of the day. They didn't like for any Jewish person to associate with Gentiles at all.) But whatever the reason, it was not good enough, because it caused even more serious problems:

> The other Jews joined him in his hypocrisy, so that by their hypocrisy even Barnabas was led astray.

First of all, because Peter was respected by other people so much, he led others to follow his example. In fact, because of the kind of respect he had earned, and because of the way people in this time thought of each other, any person who did not follow Peter's example would have been seen as insulting him. So there would be a huge problem with Peter leading other people down the wrong path.

> When I saw that they were not acting in line with the truth of the gospel, I said to Peter in front of them all, "You are a Jew, yet you live like a Gentile and not like a Jew. How is it, then, that you force Gentiles to follow Jewish customs?

Second, and more important: Jesus had changed the rules. Peter had agreed and had eaten with Gentiles. For him to stop doing this, without a good reason like not wanting to offend Jewish people he was preaching to, was a step backwards. That leads to the biggest problem of all, in 2:15-16:

> "We who are Jews by birth and not 'Gentile sinners' know that a man is not justified by observing the law, but by faith in Jesus Christ. So we, too, have put our faith in Christ Jesus that we may be justified by faith in Christ and not by observing the law, because by observing the law no one will be justified."

By refusing to eat with Gentiles, Peter was now declaring Gentiles "off limits" – contrary to Jesus. Paul points out that these Gentiles – who were Peter's fellow Christians – had been made "clean" by

Christ. What this means is that if Peter treats them as if they were "unclean," then he is denying that Jesus' work on the cross – which is what allowed people to become "clean" before God – was any good at all.

We're not saying that Peter actually thought this. Peter probably didn't realize what his actions would say to other people about Christ. Paul was just trying to get Peter to see what the implications were. Peter and Paul weren't involved in a cage match here, and there's no sign of this as something that caused Christianity to break into pieces.

Read more!

<http://www.tektonics.org/lp/petevspaul.html>

Chapter 55:

One Times Three is One

The Trinity is sometimes thought of as Christianity's weirdest and hardest to understand belief. But there's good news, and it isn't that you can save money on your car insurance by switching to a certain company. The good news is that there is an easy way to understand the Trinity.

Let's start by explaining something. There are many analogies people use to explain the Trinity (such as water being able to be liquid, solid, or gas) but none of them is perfect. There is only one that is really close, and that's this one:

- The Father is like the sun.
- Jesus is like the light from the sun.

Remember Jesus called himself the light of the world, and said that if we see him, we see the Father? Well, if you see light from a sun, you see a sun.

- The Holy Spirit is like the heat from the sun. The Spirit is how we experience God.

The reason this analogy isn't perfect is because the sun (a star) isn't a person and also isn't eternal. But the analogy does work as far as explaining the hardest part of the Trinity to understand – how the three persons are related to one another.

We can put it this way, then: Jesus and the Holy Spirit are *attributes* of the Father. Kind of like red hair or a long nose is an attribute we have; or better yet, like how intelligence can be something we have. In fact, if we look back in history and at the way the Bible describes things, what we find is that Jesus and the Spirit are described exactly that way.

Just one more thing before we explain. Today many people say "God" as though it were a personal name. This sometimes gets confusing when people say "Jesus is God" because they don't understand how one person can be another person. But in the Bible, the word used for "God" means a *type* of being – a deity – not a person's name. Today when we say "God" we usually mean the Father. But it is better and less confusing to use "God" to describe *what* the persons of the Trinity are, not *who* they are.

Now let's explain what the Bible says on this. The story actually starts in Proverbs 8, where we see a figure called *Wisdom*. The technical term for what Wisdom is, related to the Father, is a *hypostasis*. You don't need to remember that word. All you need to remember is that it means something that is an attribute of a god. It is part of that god's nature, part of the way they are.

This is very important because if Wisdom was an attribute of the Father, then that means the Father always had Wisdom. Wisdom is eternal, just like the Father. (Also notice that the word "wisdom" itself implies an attribute; just as it does for humans who have "wisdom".)

In between the time of the Old and New Testaments, Jewish authors like Sirach wrote a lot of things about this Wisdom character. They said Wisdom was eternal and was an attribute of God. You may already have guessed that this is the same thing Christianity says of Jesus.

Then, in the New Testament, we find that both Jesus and the authors of the New Testament borrowed language from Proverbs, and from authors like Sirach, to describe what Jesus was. Or to put it another way, they said that Jesus was the same person as Wisdom. Passages like John 1:1-19 and Colossians 1:15-18 are full of things which identify Jesus with the Wisdom character of Proverbs 8 and works like Sirach.

That's how we arrive at Jesus as part of the Trinity, but what about the Holy Spirit? Things are a little different here. In the Old Testament, the Spirit of God is referred to as what is used by God to create things and inspire people to do things. But in documents between the time of the Old and New Testament, the Spirit is identified as the same thing as Wisdom. Christianity revealed that Wisdom and the Spirit were not the same, but were two separate persons. However, the fact that the Spirit is seen as an attribute of God agrees with the Trinity doctrine as Christians see it.

Read more!

<http://www.tektonics.org/jesusclaims/trinitydefense.html>
<http://www.tektonics.org/qt/quietthird.html>

Chapter 56:

The Greatest Gift

We've all been taught that Jesus Christ paid for our sins when he died on the cross. But this raises two questions: *How* did he pay for our sins? And doesn't this make Christianity a "free ride" so that we can behave any way we want to as long as we're saved (or to put it another way, aren't dishonest Christians, like some televangelists, getting away with what they do because Jesus has forgiven them)?

Let's answer the first question first: *How did Jesus pay for our sins?*

If you want to use a technical term, what Jesus did was called a *vicarious sacrifice*. That's a fancy way of saying he died in our place. Many people today don't understand the idea of dying in someone else's place, even voluntarily, but ancient people thought it was an honorable thing to do, and even today, we would call someone a hero who jumped on a grenade to keep other people from being killed.

Here's a more detailed way of describing how Jesus' sacrifice of himself worked:

1. God is in the position of highest authority, of the highest good, and is therefore a being of the highest honor.
2. All sin and evil are therefore an insult to God, a disregard of His rule and authority, and also an offense to His rightful honor He receives from others.
3. Any who commit sin/evil, therefore, are taking away God honor from God that He would otherwise get from others. Because this honor rightly belongs to God, it must be restored.
4. God's proper response is to require the shaming (the opposite of honor) of those who degrade or take away His honor.
5. Jesus Christ underwent the crucifixion, a very strong experience of public shame, in our place.

Put another way, sin makes us ashamed to be in God's presence, so that we cannot be in His presence. Think of two magnets with different polarity (meaning, when you put them together, they repel each other). We're like one magnet and God is like the other. With sin in our lives, we can't stay near God; His holiness pushes us away or makes us move away, because we can't stand it. Jesus Christ is the one who changes our polarity so that we are attracted to God rather than repelled by Him.

Some may say that this seems too easy. But in reality, Christianity accomplishes the same goals as would any system of justice. When we put someone on trial for a crime, there are three purposes we usually have in mind:

1. *Punishment/restitution.* This can mean a fine, a return of property, or even a prison sentence as a way of "paying" society for the crime committed.
2. *Rehabilitation.* This means taking steps to ensure that the person does not do the crime again.
3. *Protection of the innocent.* Until #2 above is done, this is the way to keep people from being victimized further.

Christianity fulfills all three of these purposes:

1. *Punishment.* Jesus takes the punishment in our place. But, some say, this seems too easy, especially for a crooked televangelist. But not so fast. If someone (Jesus) paid for your sin when you could not afford to, then you would be indebted to that person. And the New Testament calls us servants (which means slaves) of Christ. As some teacher put it, salvation is free, but it isn't cheap. And Jesus has stern warnings for any servants of his who think they can be lazy.

2. *Rehabilitation.* We assert that God rehabilitates through the indwelling of the Spirit (in a process called *sanctification*).

3. *Protection.* Likewise, the Spirit changes people so that they will be different, and never harm others again.

None of this means that there are not Christians who will do bad things. However, it does tell us that Christians who do bad things will not just get a free pass to do what they want. Assuming they do truly believe in Jesus, Jesus promises that lazy or wicked "servants" will have to answer to him. To put it another way, a very bad Christian will get to heaven, but they will probably spend eternity scrubbing toilets in the Kingdom of God!

Read More!

<http://www.tektonics.org/af/atonedefense.html>
<http://www.christian-thinktank.com/whyjust.html>
<http://www.christian-thinktank.com/humansac.html>
<http://www.christian-thinktank.com/2littlepain.html>
<http://www.tektonics.org/uz/2muchshame.html>

Chapter 57:

Faith *Works*!

"What must I do to be saved?" A lot of Christians are confused by this question because they can't believe that we don't have to *do* something to be saved. But the Bible also has so many things in it telling us not to do wrong. So are works important or not?

The answer is yes, they are – but you do not do works *in order* to be saved. You do works *because* you are saved.

Put it this way. If you really love someone, you always do nice things for them. You buy them gifts. You show them kindness. Do you do these things to *get them* to love you, or do you do them *because* you love them?

The people of the New Testament believed that sincere belief was always followed by good works. To say otherwise is like saying water can run uphill.

Now that said, there's another reason works are important, but it isn't because of salvation. It's because of *rewards.* Jesus told many parables and said many things about servants who received rewards for their work. It is clear from what Jesus says that Christians who do good works will be *rewarded* to the extent that they have done good things. So a person who becomes a Christian, but doesn't do many good works, will be saved but may end up in the "nose-bleed seats" in heaven.

Read More!

<http://www.tektonics.org/af/baptismneed.html>

Chapter 58:

What In Hell?

The picture most people have of hell is of a place where bad people are roasting on barbeque grills while devils in red suits poke them with pitchforks. Other Christians think that the Bible teaches that the unsaved will suffer in literal flames.

But these days, as we learn more about the way the people who wrote the Bible acted and spoke, we're discovering that picture isn't quite right.

Here's a simple example. Jesus says there is fire in hell, sure (Matthew 25:41). But wait a minute. He also refers to hell as "outer darkness." (Matthew 22:13)

Fire? *And* darkness? How's that work? Are the flames black?

Elsewhere Jesus compares hell to Gehenna several times. Some Christians point out that Gehenna was a burning garbage dump outside Jerusalem, and say this points to literal flames. But have you ever seen a burning garbage dump? It doesn't flame. It smolders. It smokes. And in only a few places. Actual, visible fire is easy to avoid and is seldom seen. So if we want to take that literally, we don't have people roasting on spits either.

C. S. Lewis wrote a book titled *The Great Divorce* in which Hell is depicted as a microscopic world that is smaller than a piece of dirt in heaven (though inhabitants do not realize this except by a special "bus trip" to heaven). Within that microscopic world, people constantly get tired of the company of others and move themselves farther and farther out into the "boondocks" away from others. Lewis meant this book as an analogy, but he was closer to the truth than we may think. Remember what we said in the chapter titled, "The Greatest Gift" about how Jesus' crucifixion was about shame – not pain. Now apply this to the idea of hell. The person who is *ashamed* of their sin – because it is not paid for by Jesus — cannot come into the presence of God, but would be *driven away* from God's holiness. But God is omnipresent (everywhere), so you can't really escape it. You'd be constantly trying to run away or hide yourself, but you never can. (Remember my analogy of a magnet from the other chapter.)

But what about all those Bible verses that speak of torture, and of pain? Well, they don't. The verses people say speak of "torture" actually use the word *torment.* Physical torture is a type of torment, but there are many other kinds, such as teasing someone or being under emotional distress. The word is even used in the Bible to describe how a boat is tossed by waves. But we can see how it might be "torment" for someone to be constantly driven from God's presence, or not be able to stand it.

As for pain, that's a mistake too. Many people point to where it says there will be "weeping and gnashing of teeth" in hell. (Matthew 8:11-12, for example.) But in Jesus' time, this was not an expression of pain – it was an expression of someone who was *ashamed.*

None of this is to say that hell is a nice place to be. Even an atheist friend who liked my answers on this said that he'd prefer to not be in such a place or condition as I've described, compared to heaven. But we can certainly say that it isn't as difficult to defend the idea of hell this way.

Read More!

<http://www.tektonics.org/uz/2muchshame.html>
<http://www.christian-thinktank.com/gutripper.html>

Chapter 59:

What Is Heaven Like?

There are pictures of hell that are wrong, as we've said. There are also wrong pictures of heaven.

Many people think Heaven is all of us being turned into angels, playing harps while sitting on a cloud for eternity. Others point to pictures in Revelation of golden streets. Well, based on the last chapter, you can expect our answer to be that yes, these are metaphors too. But for what?

If hell means shame, then heaven must mean *honor*. Jesus speaks of rewards in heaven for Christians who do good works. We hear about crowns and treasures in heaven. What will that mean, practically? We're not sure. It may mean privileges, or that we get to run different parts of the universe. We just don't know. But chances are, we won't just be sitting around playing harps – more likely, we'll be put to work making things different and better.

The best book I have ever seen on this subject is by a guy named Randy Alcorn, and it is titled *Heaven*. Once you get past the first 50 pages or so, it's pretty good. Check it out.

Chapter 60:

Tomb on Empty

The question of whether Jesus rose from the dead is the one that decides whether or not Christianity is true. Paul says that if Jesus didn't rise, our faith is in vain (useless). If Jesus is still dead then you may as well quit church and join the Raelians or something. So we obviously want to be sure that Jesus *really* rose.

Both the critic and the Christian have a burden to explain how Christianity started. There are a lot of theories critics come up with to explain what happened to Jesus' body, and why the early Christians thought Jesus rose from the dead. But in the space we have, we'll just look at two of the most used: The Hallucination Theory and the Theft Theory.

The Hallucination Theory

The early Christians believed that they saw the resurrected Jesus. How can this be explained?

The most common theory of critics is that the early Christians had mass *hallucinations* of the risen Jesus. In other words, they saw something their minds imagined. Another version of this theory says they saw someone who only *looked* like Jesus and thought it was him. (There's even a guy who says that Jesus had an "evil twin" who pretended to be him!)

But there's a serious problem with this theory. According to medical experts, mass hallucinations are very rare, but they're also always based on things that the people who see the hallucination *expect* to happen. And based on the New Testament, the disciples of Jesus were not expecting Jesus to be resurrected, and didn't understand that he would be. (Matthew 16:21-2, Mark 9:9, 31; Luke 18:33, John 20:9). In addition, the Jews all expected a resurrection of all men at the end of time, but **not** one special resurrection of one man.

What were the disciples expecting, then? Based on the evidence, they were expecting Jesus' body to *ascend into heaven* – like Elijah's did, and like Moses' did, in some Jewish beliefs of that time. That means they would never have expected to see

Jesus risen from the dead. In fact, if they did ever see Jesus (or someone who looked like him), their first assumption would be that it was not Jesus, but his "guardian angel" – because the Jews of this time believed everyone had a guardian angel who looked like you. (See Acts 12:14, where everyone thinks Peter is his own angel.)

The Theft Theory

The idea that someone stole Jesus' body is the oldest theory (Matthew 28:13) and still the best one from critics, if any of them can be called good (which they can't). To make this work, critics have come up with a number of suggestions as to who might have stolen the body.

Grave Robbers. Most people who rob graves are looking for loot, not bodies. But there were a few people who broke into graves looking for bodies, and those people were what we call *necromancers*. These were magicians who needed dead bodies to cast spells. Maybe, the critics say, one of these necromancers took Jesus' body, especially thinking that since he could do miracles, his body might be very useful to them.

There are several problems with this theory. First of all, necromancy was outlawed all over the Roman Empire, and Jewish people were *especially* unfriendly to it. We also have no evidence that necromancers ever practiced anywhere near Jewish lands.

Second, it is hard to explain why necromancers would go out of their way to get a body out of a tomb like Jesus' – with a one ton rock in front of it, and right next to a busy urban area like Jerusalem, where they'd have to drag a body through – when they could dig one up anywhere, out in the country, from the ground. "But Jesus was a holy man! They may have wanted his body because of that," a critic may say. But we pointed out in other chapters that Jesus was badly shamed when he was crucified. He would no longer be regarded as a holy man, but as one who had lost his power (and holiness).

(Spells also required a lot of other weird stuff – like a drowned field mouse, baboon dung, or the eggs of an ibis. Unfortunately, you couldn't just get those at the local Wal-Mart.)

Third, all evidence shows that necromancers *never stole whole bodies*. They did one of two things: They either left something with the body, or cut off part of the body (like a nose or an ear) and took it with them, leaving the rest. (So what would the Gospel message be? "His nose is Risen"?) The only time people ever stole whole bodies from graves was when they stole mummies from Egyptian tombs because it was thought that some of the stuff used to preserve the mummies had a medical use – but that didn't start happening until 1000 years after Jesus.

The Apostles. By far, though, as in Matthew, the followers of Jesus are the major suspects for a theft of the body. After all, they knew where the body was, and had a motive, right?

True, but that's not enough to convict on a crime, or else most of us would be in jail right now. Are the disciples good suspects otherwise? Not really. As is often pointed out, to have stolen Jesus' body would mean risking persecution (sometimes even death) for a lie. And because claiming that Jesus rose from the dead would be a direct challenge to what the ruling powers had decided about Jesus, and because their claims were contrary to what everyone believed (see the chapter, "Culture Shock"), the disciples would be given the "third degree" by everyone who heard their claims.

We can add one more obvious argument: The tomb was guarded. Okay, the critic says; that story was just made up. It's only in Matthew, and no one else mentions it. Or maybe they stole Jesus' body before the guard could get out there.

Those answers won't work either. True, there was no one *assigned by Pilate* to guard the tomb until the priests came to see him. But the suspicion of the priests that Jesus' disciples would steal the body didn't start at just that moment before they went to Pilate. And the priests had thousands of Temple workers at their disposal who would jump when they said "go." It would actually be absurd to suppose that they did *not* have someone watching the tomb (even if from afar) from the very start – even if they were just unarmed, untrained gofers who would observe from hiding and report anything suspicious.

And there's one more thing, and it explains why only Matthew mentions the guard. We've already pointed out that Jesus' death was shameful. Well, strange as it seems, his burial was too. You're probably scratching your head – *wasn't Joseph of Arimathea a follower of Jesus?* Why would being buried in his tomb be shameful? Well, because people were supposed to be buried *with or near* their families. To be buried in a stranger's tomb was shameful. Joseph may have been trying to make the best of it, but no matter what he did, burial in his tomb for Jesus would have looked bad on Jesus.

The point being: As part of shaming people in burial, especially executed criminals, the authorities did not allow the family to mourn and perform mourning rites at the tomb. Now Jesus was a public figure with a lot of followers. So the authorities knew a lot of people might show up to mourn. So one reason for the tomb to be guarded was *to prevent mourning by Jesus' followers*. This would then explain why Matthew is the only one to record the guard: Because the guard was actually a very embarrassing thing to Jesus. The only reason Matthew mentions it is to answer claims of theft – which none of the other Gospels had to do.

People we have answers to on this:

- Richard Carrier

Read More!

<http://www.tektonics.org/tomb/emptytomb.html>
<http://www.tektonics.org/guest/wildvis.html>

James Patrick Holding, *The Impossible Faith* (Xulon Press, 2006).

Chapter 61:

Insert Prayer, Get Gumball

In Matthew 21:21-22, Jesus says that if we have faith, we can move mountains with prayer. In Matthew 18:19 he says that if two of us agree on anything, we can ask for anything. And 1 John 5:14-15 says that we can ask anything according to his will, and he'll hear us.

Okay. I just asked for a Cadillac. Where is it?

Hmm. I still have an old clunker in my garage. Why?

Let's find out why, by looking at these verses.

Matthew 18:19 – First, as always, context is important, and let's see in what context this verse has:

> Matthew 18:15-20 "If your brother sins against you, go and show him his fault, just between the two of you. If he listens to you, you have won your brother over. But if he will not listen, take one or two others along, so that every matter may be established by the testimony of two or three witnesses. If he refuses to listen to them, tell it to the church; and if he refuses to listen even to the church, treat him as you would a pagan or a tax collector. I tell you the truth, whatever you bind on earth will be bound in heaven, and whatever you loose on earth will be loosed in heaven. Again, I tell you that if two of you on earth agree about anything you ask for, it will be done for you by my Father in heaven. For where two or three come together in my name, there am I with them."

We can see from this that Matthew 18:19 isn't a general instruction on how to pray for whatever you want. It is instructions for pursuing "sheep" (members of the believing community, that is, other Christians) who go astray. Verses 15-18 are further instructions for community discipline. Verse 19 is only about discipline in the body of Christ, and God recognizing their decision as valid where two or more people agree on the discipline used against the straying Christian.

Matthew 21:21-22 (also Matthew 7:7-8, John 14:13-14) — This one might seem to be more of a problem, but let's talk about reality here: How realistic is it to think that this is *really* a license to overturn mountains? Is it logical to think that God wanted us to be able to mess things up that much? Not really. Here's what it actually is all about.

In Mark 6:23, Herod wants to give a reward to his step-daughter, and he says she can have up to "half his kingdom." Now in Jesus' time, people didn't say this sort of thing because they meant it **literally**. It was a way of saying, "I'm very grateful." The *last* thing the girl would have done was to say, "Okay, I'll take the north half." That would have been rude and obnoxious.

"Moving mountains" was a Jewish metaphor for doing difficult things. It is Jesus' way of saying, "This is how much God is concerned with you." Only a small number of people were considered righteous enough to ask for and receive whatever they wanted — and because they were righteous, they weren't going around asking for just *anything* they wanted, but only what they supposed to be in the will of God.

So what are we supposed to ask for? The Lord's Prayer (Matthew 6), which was a model Jesus left for prayer, has us asking only for daily needs like food and water. Not cars or money or even a cell phone. Not even special healings. Just basic needs.

Promises like Herod's and Jesus' were made with the full understanding that they were dramatic hyperbole, not an ironclad, literal guarantee. Like the guy in the chapter, "How the Bible Talks To You" who offers to let you burn his house, it is a way of saying something else less dramatic. You would hardly say, if the man didn't actually want you to burn his house down, that he was being unwelcoming; so there is no way to say that unless God fulfills these "prayer promises" literally, He must be unloving or breaking His promise.

That leaves to **1 John 5:14-15**, and you'll notice that John added the qualifying phrase, "according to his will." John wrote to people who were Gentiles. A qualifier like that would have been unnecessary for Jesus' Jewish audience. It would go without saying that that mountain (even a literal one) would go nowhere without God's approval implied.

Read More!

<http://www.tektonics.org/lp/prayfor.html>

Chapter 62:

You Are Now Being Served

In church, a pastor or minister is sometimes called a "worship leader". This would seem to mean that "worship" has to do with singing or praying only. But if we look up the word and what it means in the Bible, we find that "worship" is much more than this.

"Worship" was a human reaction to awareness of the way God was: holy, righteous, just, and merciful. The reaction was always expressed in the presence of God, but God's presence was not required for it to happen. It was also a reaction to God's acts in history to help His people.

Elsewhere in the Bible, the word is used to refer to bowing down before leaders or superiors. It does not necessarily mean that you liked the person you were "worshipping". It just meant you were submitting to them and acknowledging that they had authority, and that you would do whatever they told you to do. Worship therefore means serving God in all kinds of different ways – not just singing or praise (which is just one type of worship).

Many people think "worship" is all about making you feel better. But it is clear from the Bible that worship is a *life and lifestyle*, not just acts in isolated pockets of time. Worship today can mean serving in a soup kitchen, or going on a mission trip, or conducting a ministry of some sort. In fact, you might say that something like that is closer to Biblical "worship" than singing songs in church!

Read More!

<http://www.tektonics.org/whatis/whatworship.html>

Chapter 63:

Bible Dictionary

Paul spoke of *faith*, *hope* and *love* as three great things in the life of a Christian. But what exactly are each of these three things? It just so happens that today we have a few wrong ideas about them. What these three words meant in Paul's time is a little different than what we sometimes think they mean. And that's important, because often critics of Christianity have the same kind of wrong ideas.

Faith

Let's start with faith. Here are three examples of how we hear that word used today:

1. A "faith healer" offers to heal Joe of his acne. He lays hands on Joe and prays, but the acne remains. He waves Joe away, saying, "This is your problem. You don't have enough *faith*."
2. A Christian faces several objections to his beliefs that he cannot answer. He says, "I don't care what people say, I still have *faith*."

3. The famous skeptic Mark Twain said, "*Faith* is believing what you know ain't so."

The problem is that all three of these examples offer an incorrect definition or understanding of what Biblical *faith* is all about. The Greek word behind "faith" in the New Testament is *pistis*. As a noun, *pistis* is a word that was sometimes used as a term for *proof*. There's an example of this in the New Testament in Acts 17:31:

> For he has set a day when he will judge the world with justice by the man he has appointed. He has given **proof** of this to all men by raising him from the dead.

The raising of Christ is spoken of here as a *proof* that God will judge the world. Proof was a very important part of preaching in Acts. Check the speeches of Peter and Paul and you will see that they appeal to the evidence of miracles, especially the resurrection of Jesus, and also how Jesus fulfilled the prophecy of the Old Testament. People were expected to have faith *because of* these proofs.

What this tells us is that "faith" isn't blind. *Pistis* in fact meant *faithfulness*, or *loyalty* as owed to someone who had earned it. "Faith" is not a feeling, but our pledge to trust, and be reliable servants to, our God, who has provided us with the gifts of forgiveness of sins through Christ, as proven by miracles and prophecy.

Let's now look at a couple of passages understanding "faith" to mean loyalty.

> Mark 6:5-6 He could not do any miracles there, except lay his hands on a few sick people and heal them. And he was amazed at their lack of faith.

Some people quote this verse and say that it indicates that Jesus was like a modern "faith healer" who excuses away their inability to heal real diseases as a lack of faith by the sick person. The word "unbelief" here is *apistia*, meaning a lack of *pistis*. Once we understand this to mean lack of loyalty, we see that the problem is not with Jesus but with the lack of trust by those who rejected Jesus. They were ungrateful, even though he had done good things for them – and even today we don't like to give things to people who are ungrateful!

Let's look at one other verse, the one that many people have in mind when they use Twain's definition:

> Hebrews 11:1 Now faith is being sure of what we hope for and certain of what we do not see.

"There, see! The evidence of things not seen. Blind faith. Case closed." Try again! The list that follows in Hebrews offers examples of people who had been given *undeniable proof* of God's existence and power. *Pistis* was trust in a God who has demonstrated His ability to be a worthy leader, and the examples in Hebrews are those of followers of God who, knowing this ability, *trust* in God's record as a provider. Hebrews 11:1 therefore is telling us that *faith* (trust in God, gained by conviction based on evidence) is the *substance* (the word here means an assurance) of things *hoped for* (this word means *expected* by trust, which is something earned! – see next entry), and the evidence of that which is not seen, which in context means:

We expect, based on past performance, *continuing favor from our God*, who has already proven Himself worthy of our trust by example, and this trust is our confidence in the fulfillment of future promises. Blind faith? Not in the least! It is faith grounded in reality.

Hope

Hope is another word that is sometimes misunderstood. In Acts 24:16, Paul says (I'll have to use the King James Version here):

> And have hope toward God, which they themselves also allow, that there shall be a resurrection of the dead, both of the just and unjust.

Today we say things like, "I hope my team wins the Super Bowl" and it implies that we don't think they might because it would be very hard, but we want them to. So some think that here Paul is saying that he doesn't think there will be a resurrection, but he wants there to be one! But the word "hope" in the New Testament doesn't mean this. The Greek word is *elpis*, meaning to *anticipate* or *expect*.

Hope in the Bible is therefore the act of placing allegiance in a trustworthy and reliable source. And so, the verse above means that Paul *believes firmly* that God will resurrect all persons. It reflects his *security*, not his uncertainty.

Love

This last word is sometimes read as having to do with hearts and flowers and candy, or at least being nice to other people. Some also try to say it means we don't confront others with sin. But that's not quite what it is.

The word used for "love" is *agape*. Our culture (most of you who read this will be in America or one of the other "Western" nations) is centered on the *individual*, whereas ancient Biblical society (and 70% of societies today) are *group*-centered. In other words, people in these types of societies believe that what is good for the group is what is most important.

Because of this, *agape* would not have had anything to do with feelings, but had to do with looking out for the best interests of the **most** people. And this may sometimes mean hurting one person so that the greater number of people will not be hurt.

If you've ever seen the movie *Lean on Me*, you saw a perfect example of *agape* love. The high school principal Joe Clark cleaned out his high school and made it a safe place for those who wanted to learn. He kicked out anyone who disrupted the learning of others. He used physical compulsion to do it as needed. He used a bullhorn to get people's attention. This was *agape* because Clark valued what was best for his students as a whole versus what a few of them wanted at the expense of others.

Read More!

<http://www.tektonics.org/whatis/whatfaith.html>
<http://www.tektonics.org/whatis/whathope.html>
<http://www.tektonics.org/whatis/whatlove.html>

Grab Bag

Last part. I just picked a few questions at random out of a hat and decided to answer them. Luckily I stopped before I got to one of those "truth or dare" questions.

Chapter 64:

When Bad Stuff Happens

It's a really old question that's been talked over for centuries: *If God exists and is good, why is there so much evil?*

In a small book like this, there's no way we can do justice to such a big question. But we can give you some food for thought.

Christians believe that God has taken care of evil. Of course, we can say that God **has** done something about evil – he sent Jesus to die on the cross, and will someday finish the job by destroying evil after all who can be saved, will be. The only real question is, "Why doesn't God do it *now*?" I can ask a question back: "What makes you think *now* is the best time to do it?" To know the answer to that, you'd have to be God. The person who asks this doesn't see past their own experience. They also probably don't act perfect themselves. Chances are they don't really want God to stop all evil now, because they'd have to go too.

Here's an even better reply. If this person is so concerned with evil, why aren't *they* out stopping it right now? They may say, "But I'm not omnipotent like God is supposed to be!" True. But they have *some* power. And by their logic, if they're not doing something to stop all the evil they can *right now*, then they're hypocrites for asking God to do it all right now. No one really wants all evil stopped right now – just the parts of it that they're not involved in!

Even so, why should we assume God isn't doing things to stop evil now? And how would someone who asks a question like that know better? A friend of mine told a story of a man who objected that God could not exist, because innocent babies sometimes die. Later the same person objected to the Holocaust. "Why couldn't God have killed Hitler when he was a baby and avoided it all?" he asked. My friend pointed out an obvious problem: If baby Hitler had died mysteriously, the man would use the other objection, "why do innocent babies die," to object to it!

Most evil is caused by us. God did do something else about the problem of evil – he sent us to control it and stop it. But we just don't do a good job sometimes, even by ourselves. A murderer often becomes a murderer because other people (society) failed him. Many diseases happen to us because we don't take care of ourselves the way we should and eat too many fattening foods, or we smoke, or drink.

All sin breaks God's laws. If we sin, we don't have a lot we can say to God about Him not stopping evil.

We can't even keep our own house in order! When we sin, too, we tell God, "Don't tell me what to do." Isn't it kind of ungrateful to do this, then demand that God step in just when we want Him to?

The tsunami that happened in 2004 is often used as an example of evil that God should have stopped. But there were ways that we could have avoided the results of it. Many nations could have had earthquake-detection and tsunami warning equipment, but spent the money on something else instead. And God actually already left "early warnings" – it's a well known fact that animals were seen fleeing inland before the tsunami hit. How they knew what was coming we aren't sure. But it is clear that God has not left us without ways to avoid disasters.

There is much more good than there is evil. Bad things hit us very hard as individuals, and we shouldn't make less of them than we do. But if we measure the sum total of all human experience, there's much more good in the world than there is evil.

Once again, let's use the tsunami as an example. Yes, it was a terrible disaster. But let's take a longer look: For every tsunami, there are thousands of natural events that are beautiful or beneficial, not harmful. For every Hurricane Katrina, there are thousands of rain storms that help us grow crops and feed people. Sometimes we watch the news and think there's too much evil, but the news doesn't cover good things most of the time. It's hard to get an accurate picture of the whole when the camera only shows a little bit!

Read More!

<http://www.christian-thinktank.com/gutripper.html>

Chapter 65:

Guilt by Association

> "Christians are _________. That's why I wouldn't be one."

Fill in the blank however you like. "Hypocrites" is said a lot. So is "self-righteous." Or even "ignorant." I've seen that one a lot. Or maybe even, "the ones who killed millions of people in the Spanish Inquisition." (We'll talk about that one later.)

But whatever you put in there, it's the same thing: Guilt by association. And that's a fallacy – the Hasty Generalization, as we said. (It would be too, by the way, if you put something *good* in there, and said, "That's why I *would* be one.")

But anyway, let's expand on why this is a fallacy. Christianity is based on a claim that Jesus rose from the dead. Okay. How does the fact that Joe Christian is a hypocrite change that? This is like claiming that you don't believe the North won the Civil War because a person you met from New York was mean to you. Or that the theory of evolution was wrong because Richard Dawkins got caught shoplifting. (He wasn't, by the way. That's just an example.)

This would only matter if, for example, Christianity *taught* people to be hypocrites. But it doesn't. Jesus condemns hypocrisy. What people do *in spite of* what they believe teaches, doesn't count against the validity of what they believe.

This is not to say we shouldn't worry about what people see in us. Sometimes we're still a "gateway" for people to want to learn more. But when you have someone who won't let go of an argument like this one, you're better off talking to someone else if they won't listen to reason. (Or as Jesus would say, shake the dust from your feet.)

Chapter 66:

The Tolerance Trap

Any time you start talking about Christianity, someone is bound to say, "It's intolerant to claim that Christianity is the only way to be saved."

Sometimes this isn't used as a real argument, but is used to cut off conversation because the person can't answer your arguments. But other times it is meant seriously. Unfortunately, there are several problems with making it as a point.

Tolerance doesn't mean not correcting errors. Imagine getting a bad grade on a test, and telling the professor, "But you should be more tolerant of my answers and not mark them wrong." You're not likely to get a better grade that way (but you might get a chuckle from the professor). Now of course, some will say, "That's a test. We're talking about religion." But who decided that religion was exempt from tests of truth?

Tolerance doesn't account for contradictions. Related to the first point, it can't be denied that religions contradict each other in main beliefs. Islam contradicts Hinduism as far as how many gods exist (one versus millions). Clearly one or the other is right, or both are wrong, but both can't be right.

"Tolerance" put this way isn't tolerant. When someone tells you to be "tolerant" because you're saying someone is wrong, then they're being *intolerant* of your view that someone is wrong. If tolerance means never saying someone is wrong, then the person accusing you can't say you're wrong either.

In truth, "tolerance" doesn't mean never saying anyone is wrong. It means, basically, putting up with something you may not like. It has to do with experience, not truth.

Chapter 67:

No One Expects a Defense

The Spanish Inquisition! This one is popular among critics who pair it with the Crusades (see the next chapter) as an example of how Christianity has ruined Western culture and kept us from becoming heart-cutting, human-sacrificing enlightened people like the Aztecs. The Spanish Inquisition, they say, killed millions and terrorized people right and left. How about we dig for some truth on this one?

Where was the Inquisition? Spain was only one place where an Inquisition occurred; it actually started with events in France. It eventually spread all over Western Europe in a lot of forms and for a lot of purposes, then gradually died out, lasting at the latest until 1808 in Spain.

Why was there an Inquisition? The simple answer is that the Inquisition was seen as a means of *social survival* – something people needed in order for society to function. At the time of the Inquisition, the Catholic Church was the one thing that provided leadership and order and kept society from falling into disorder and despair. This was more than the church was supposed to do, but unfortunately, the church was the only institution with the means and the motive to do it.

Threats to the church were therefore seen as a threat to the physical, mental, and spiritual well-being of everyone else. But then along came a group called the Cathars, who taught that Satan was the creator of the material world, and that Satan made man, and that God felt sorry for man and gave him a soul. The Cathars also taught poverty, vegetarianism, honesty, and abstention. Not a bad mix of principles at the end, and had they kept to themselves nobody probably would have bothered them.

But then the Cathars decided that the Catholic Church was a tool of Satan that tricked Christians into thinking they were saved, and they didn't stay quiet about it. And this was like laying bombs under the Capitol building in Washington today.

The society of this time did not yet have the leisure to allow such powerful dissent and yet still be able to survive. The Inquisition's actions would be excessive today because we have the leisure to tolerate dissent with no threat to our survival. They didn't have that choice yet. And so, there was an Inquisition.

What was the "quiz" in "Inquisition"? The word "inquisition" implies questions, and at first, that was all the Inquisition did – ask questions. Some monks were sent to France to check up on the

Cathars. Unfortunately, the Cathars wouldn't cooperate and tried to hide themselves. Then the Cathars made a big mistake: They killed one of the Pope's special representatives. After that it became harder to accept that they'd be able to be left alone.

And so, the Inquisition changed tactics. Everyday people were asked to look for heretics and turn them in for punishment. What kind of punishment? Not execution, no, not at first. They would be excommunicated (cut off) from the church, and then turned over to the state to be banished and/or have the property taken away. These were normal ways people were punished back then.

Over the next 25 years the Inquisition worked in France, and followed a typical procedure which was also roughly followed in Spain:

1. One or more inquisitors arrived at a town or village and preached against the heresy.
2. They offered a *grace period* of 7 to 30 days for heretics to repent and get a light sentence. Now here, unfortunately, some people took it on themselves to abuse the system. Some everyday people would report their neighbors as heretics just to cause them trouble, because of something else they didn't like (such as maybe that they had a loud goat who brayed at 3 AM). People used the Inquisition to get back at other people. Also unfortunately, legal standards of evidence were not as good as they are today, so innocent people were often accused unjustly. But this also happened in

regular courts of the day, so it wasn't particularly the Inquisition's problem.

3. After the grace period anyone suspected of heresy was brought before a group of judges and asked to confess. If the confession did not match what had been reported about them by others, they went to prison where they were advised to think it over. The same was done to those who protested their innocence. Following this, various methods were used to gain a confession, including intense questioning, pleas from family members, and at the extreme end, starvation and torture. Blame Christianity? No — this was actually how the legal system worked as far back as Rome's time. (Of course, even today we have debates over whether it is right to use torture on people like terrorists, and we won't decide that question here.)

   Once a confession was made, punishment ranged from fasting and prayer (the equal to writing "I will not be a heretic" on the blackboard 100 times) to a brief imprisonment. Those who had committed serious crimes were given life imprisonment. Execution was reserved only those who would not repent, or who went back into heresy after repenting before.

What about the torture? The shame of the Inquisition is the use of torture, and we won't explore the details of how they did it, but here, human nature caused the worst of the problems. Torturers were only allowed to torture a prisoner once, but got around the rule by "suspending" a torture session until the next day to continue it. On the other hand, compared to methods used by the *secular* legal system of the day — which included being burned alive for counterfeiting and execution for thievery, and later being disemboweled or boiled to death — the Inquisition wasn't as serious a threat to health and well-being as its secular counterparts. One of its worst practices was executing someone, then publicly burning their remains, and confiscating their property, leaving their family — even if they were not heretics — bankrupt. Imprisonment may have been the most cruel of the Inquisition's penalties. Like in all ancient jails, cells were cramped and unlit, so that prisoners at times could neither lie down nor stand, and a lot of people died in jails. (On the other hand, the Inquisition's jails were so much better than the secular jails that one person in a secular jail said something heretical so he could be transferred to the Inquisition jail!)

How many people were killed? Without minimizing the bad things done by the Inquisition, it is a fact that many critics exaggerate its deeds. I have heard some say that the Inquisition killed "millions" of people. But the fact is that in Spain and all the land it owned, at least, no more than two thousand people were actually executed by the Inquisition. ("Millions" would be hard anyway, since the population of Spain was only about 7 million back then.) And torture, despite the horror of it, was only rarely used. Given how bad secular courts were for using torture and painful execution methods, we may as well credit Christianity for making the Inquisition *less* severe than it would have been had it been run by secular authorities addressing the same social fears and concerns! Prison sentences were often not literally observed; a "life sentence" could amount to only ten years and the term could be served at home, in a monastery, or in a hospital when prison space was limited. Plus there were many places where people never saw or even *ignored* the Inquisition.

Once again, we shouldn't minimize the bad things that happened during the Inquisition. But we also shouldn't blow them way out of proportion, as some critics do.

Read More!

<http://www.tektonics.org/qt/spaninq.html>

Chapter 68:

I Love a Crusade

From the way some critics talk about the Crusades, you might think that it was a bunch of evil, barbaric Christians who went off into other countries and chopped the heads off of innocent people who were minding their own business and picking flowers at the time. The recent movie *Kingdom of Heaven* wasn't as bad as that, but it still managed to not tell the whole story.

Of course, we're not saying Christians were all squeaky-clean when it comes to the Crusades, but it's a good idea to put the whole thing into some historical perspective! Soldiers go overboard and commit atrocities in any war. And there's nothing about Christianity that teaches us to do things like that, or allows us to do things like that.

The main myth to be busted here is the one that says that Crusader Christians barged in on a bunch of peaceful people and tried to convert them or kill them. That's not what the Crusades were about. The Crusades started because at the time, for the past several hundred years, Muslims had been gradually conquering (by war) many territories inhabited by Christians, including the Holy Land (what is now basically Israel). Sadly, these conquerors committed many atrocities against innocent people in those areas (whether they were Muslim or Christian!), and also were forcibly trying to convert Christians to Islam. In addition, many Christians went as pilgrims (you might say, tourists) to the Holy Land, from all over Europe, and the conquerors were harassing them also, sometimes even killing them.

The Crusades were started because Christians were trying to protect other Christians who were being hurt or killed. Sadly, in many cases the Crusaders attacked innocent people on the way, including other Christians. There were also many serious mistakes made by the Crusaders. For example, when they did arrive at Jerusalem on the First Crusade, they didn't know that it had been taken over, while they were on their way, by Muslims who would have been more likely to let Christian pilgrims travel without being bothered – but when they found out, they decided to try to take it over anyway! On the other hand, the Crusaders didn't just kill anyone and everyone in the city, as some critics like to say.

There were several different Crusades, and each one turned out differently. The Third Crusade, for example, ended with peaceful and successful negotiations, not a bloody war. But either way, there's often more fiction than truth in how movies like *The Kingdom of Heaven* portray the Crusades.

Read More!

Daniel Hoffman, "*The Kingdom of Heaven* and the Real Crusades," *Christian Research Journal* 29 (3), 2006.

Chapter 69:

To The Shores of Tripoli

There's a paragraph found in a treaty reached with certain Muslim pirates of the African coast at Tripoli, one part of which, Article 11, says:

> As the government of the United States of America is **not in any sense founded on the Christian Religion**,-as it has in itself no character of enmity against the laws, religion

> or tranquility of Musselmen,-and as the said States never have entered into any war or act of hostility against any Mehomitan nation, it is declared by the parties that no pretext arising from religious opinions shall ever produce an interruption of the harmony existing between the two countries.

For a long time the "Christian Religion" part of this was being passed around, falsely said to be a saying of George Washington, but although that's usually been corrected, the phrase does appear in the treaty and it is used to claim that America wasn't influenced in its founding by Christian principles. But is that what it really means?

We don't have room to discuss the whole big issue of what Christianity had to do with America's origins, but we can refute the use of this Article 11, at least. Yes, it is in the treaty, and the treaty was approved by Congress and signed by the President (who was John Adams at the time, not Washington). The first thing we need to do is look at two dates connected to the treaty:

- January 4, 1797 – copy of the treaty certified by America's representative
- April 10, 1799 – settlement delivered in Tripoli

Notice that the time span is significant – over *two years.*

Now we need to look more deeply into what this treaty was all about. Basically, Muslim pirates associated with Muslim states on the coast of Africa – such as Tripoli, Tunis, and Algiers – were capturing merchant ships from other countries and holding the crews for ransom. They had been doing this for more than 300 years, and most countries found it easiest to just pay the ransoms. The ships they attacked were always ships from countries that were mainly populated by Christians. For the pirates, this was a religious war, not just a war for money.

Originally, America paid the ransoms just like any other country. They could have fought them, but the problem was that certain European countries actually *wanted* the pirates to stay around, because they helped eliminate business competition from other countries, including America! Also, America just wasn't that strong yet, and was worried about a possible war with France.

In this situation, any time a treaty was delayed meant there would be more piracy, more being at war with the pirates, and more possibilities of innocent Americans being captured and sold into slavery, and more economic burdens for businesses in America. With no help coming from other countries, and with treaties taking so long to negotiate and send back and forth across the ocean — what would the American government be expected to do? Even if anyone objected to Article 11, it would have been foolish to send it back for re-negotiation. It would be more important to get the treaty through than to rework it.

But there's two more important points. First, when the treaty was renegotiated 8 years later, Article 11 wasn't in it any more. By that time, America had more of an upper hand and was in a position to give the pirates the shorter end of the stick. This tells us that the reworking of the treaty without Article 11 better reflects American beliefs than the earlier version. Second, no other treaty America signed with the other Muslim pirate states contains anything like Article 11.

By now you may be wondering how Article 11 got into the treaty in the first place. Well, we're not sure. It sounds like it may have been written by one of the pirates' leaders when they composed their version of it in Arabic. If that's the case, then Article 11 means even less than we would think, because to the pirates, "not founded on the Christian religion" would mean that America was not a Christian theocracy, or a state where the church had political power, as the religious authorities in Muslim nations had power. It doesn't mean that America's people and government were not influenced by Christian morals or principles.

Read More!

<http://www.tektonics.org/qt/tripoli.html>

Chapter 70:

Whacked on the Head with a Telescope

Another historical event this time – one that's always brought up to show how "anti-science" Christians have always been. In 1632, the astronomer

Galileo was convicted of heresy, supposedly because he taught that the earth was not the center of the universe, which was supposed to be contrary to the Bible. By now you know I wouldn't bring this up if there weren't some missing facts, so what are they?

This was not science vs. religion - it was Aristotle vs. Copernicus. The reason most people in Galileo's day – including astronomers! — believed that the earth was the center of the universe was not because they thought it was the teaching of the Bible, but because of the ancient Greek astronomer Aristotle. It was another astronomer before Galileo, Copernicus (1473-1543), who first challenged this idea.

Unfortunately, many (not all) people in the church, like everyone else, liked what Aristotle had to say better, and wrongly connected any disproof of Aristotle with a disproof of Christianity. But the church called on other astronomers who were Aristotelians for support, and they used information from them to validate how they read the Bible – and it was these other astronomers who cast the first stone at Galileo, not the church. (Before then, Galileo was held in favor by the church and was even given a special audience with the Pope.)

Galileo himself was a Christian. This seems to slide right by when critics present Galileo as a defender of truth versus bigoted religion. Galileo was a firm believer in the truth of the Bible, though he did think people misunderstood it to support Aristotle. (See the chapter, "Flat Earth, Solid Sky" for related examples.) He tried to show that the Bible was compatible with the theory that the earth revolved around the sun.

Unfortunately, Galileo was also someone who didn't know how to make his case politely. He made many enemies by using insulting language against people he disagreed with, and he sometimes attacked people who questioned his findings. This probably contributed significantly to his arrest and trial.

Read More!

<http://www.christiananswers.net/q-eden/galileo.html>
<http://www.creationontheweb.com/content/view/3006>

Chapter 71:

Mega Book Burning!

In earlier chapters we talked about how many copies of the New Testament we have from ancient times, especially compared to other documents. But that brings up something else: Is it the fault of Christians that we don't have copies of these other documents? In fact, didn't Christians burn a lot of pagan literature and libraries – maybe even to hide the truth that Christianity was a fraud?

The answer is that while we can find isolated examples of Christians burning books, for the *most part* we find that church leaders were intent on *preserving and appreciating* pagan literature. Even what they disagreed with, you may ask? No, that would be an exception. For example, they didn't have any interest in copying works by critics of Christianity like Celsus or Porphyry. But neither did they go out on scavenger hunts trying to find copies so they could burn them. Ultimately the real reason we don't have some ancient books today is that no one was interested enough in them to make copies. (The fact that books decayed quickly, and that there were invasions by barbarians who used books as napkins, didn't help much either.)

Burning or destroying books was not a Christian idea. Long before Jesus, and long after, the Romans would burn books belonging to groups they considered deviants. Some of their actions were against Christians. But actual examples of Christians returning the favor are relatively rare.

The most famous claimed example of Christian book-burning alleges that Christians destroyed a famous library at Alexandria, in Egypt. One critic says that in the year 391, Christians burned over 700,000 books. This is false. The library had been badly damaged, yes – but by *pagan* soldiers in a battle ninety years before Jesus lived! More damage was done to the library in another battle about 40 years later. In 273 A.D., Aurelian – a pagan emperor who disliked Christianity – burned most of Alexandria, and more destruction was performed by another pagan emperor, Diocletian, a few years later.

Did Christians actually destroy any of the library at Alexandria? Yes – in 391, they did destroy a very small library that was part of a larger pagan temple, and this was only because some pagans had holed up in it using it as a military bunker. (They had also captured some Christians and were torturing them inside the temple.)

To be sure, over history, the church has burned books or banned them for various reasons. But actions like that have been occasional, not systematic. To claim that Christians were on a widespread campaign to destroy ancient pagan literature is simply false.

People we have answers to who make these claims:

- Helen Ellerbee

Read More!

<http://www.christian-thinktank.com/qburnbx.html>

Chapter 72:

Pass the Collection Plate!

When I was in college, it seemed that every month it made news about some "televangelist" (television evangelist) being found guilty of something immoral. Sometimes, but not always, part of what they did wrong had to do with the way they misused money that had been donated to their ministry. Maybe the most famous example was that of Jim Bakker, who was especially criticized for buying air-conditioned houses for his dogs. Other Christian leaders have been criticized for paying themselves salaries that are much too high.

When Christian leaders misuse money, we should always be ready to call them down for it. But some take this too far and act like Christian leaders are always (or usually) "in it for the money." And then it goes so far that churches are criticized for just passing a collection plate.

Let's look at this realistically. Churches *do* need money to operate and conduct ministry. Ministers do deserve compensation of some kind (as Jesus says, the worker is worth his wages – Luke 10:7). And we have plenty of charitable organizations out there that operate the same way. At the same time, we also see people objecting any time any of these groups asks for money (like public television), and we also hear about scandals in secular charities (for example, one leader of United Way was recently accused of misusing the charity's assets for himself). But who would say that this proves all or even most people working for charities are "in it for the money"? Even atheist organizations ask for and receive money. I even know of some that sell things like T-shirts and cookbooks to raise funds.

Abuse of money is a human problem, not a Christian problem. We should always watch out for and penalize those who abuse the trust we put in them. Christians are no exception. But the person who uses this as an argument against Christianity just isn't being rational.

Chapter 73:

The Mirror Crack'd

Depending on who you talk to, you may find that the words "Christian" and "hypocrite" are basically synonyms!

What is a hypocrite, exactly? It means a person who pretends to have virtue but doesn't. Put another way, they say, "Do as I say, not as I do."

There are hypocrites everywhere, in all religions and in all places. But Christians seem to get tagged with that word a lot. Why? Sometimes it is because people assume that anyone who sticks up for morality *must* be a hypocrite. It can be just an easy insult to throw around.

But one reason Christians are targets so much is, well – because we stick out more. We evangelize. We are given our example by Jesus, who stood up for the right thing. And sadly, because many of us *do* commit hypocrisy. We act holy only on Sunday, not every day. We don't reflect Christ as we should.

Naturally, the same as with other things we have talked about in this book, the fact that any or all Christians are hypocrites doesn't have any bearing on whether or not Jesus rose from the dead, which is what makes Christianity true. Truly, people should question the *sincerity* of our beliefs, not our beliefs, when they see us being hypocrites. But unfortunately, that's a false impression we're always going to have to deal with.

Chapter 74:

No Wine Before Its Time

Depending on where you go to church, you may have heard different things about whether it is okay for a Christian to drink alcohol. I can give a couple of major contrasts: The Southern Baptist church I attend would really disapprove of alcohol and would never serve it with church meals on Wednesday night. But when I went to speak at a Catholic church once, they were having a dinner, and the first thing I was asked was, "Would you like some wine or beer with your dinner?" What a difference!

For me, alcohol isn't a big temptation because I just don't like it very much. But if you're wondering what the Bible has to say on the subject, you may get a little confused. Sometimes you find it saying people shouldn't drink, and it condemns drunkenness. Other times it seems to show drinking alcohol in a good way. So how can we figure this out?

There are a couple of things we need to realize first. These days, any of us can go down to the Jiffy food store and buy a six-pack of beer, or a bottle of vodka, for a really cheap price. It wasn't that way in Bible times. Alcoholic drinks were much harder to make and were very expensive. People usually only had alcohol at big festivals, unless they were rich (which explains why a lot of warnings against alcohol in the Bible come from the works of Solomon, like Proverbs). And as you might guess, that would have made it harder to drink enough to get drunk.

Not only that, but alcoholic drinks were nowhere near as strong as the ones we can find today at the convenience store. So you'd have to drink a lot more of their drinks if you wanted to get drunk.

I needed to explain all of this so I could give a more complete answer. The Bible doesn't ever say we **can't** drink alcohol (except that *some* people in positions of authority, like priests, are told not to). The Bible does, however, say we shouldn't get drunk. But if we leave it at that, we won't get a complete picture unless we know how different their alcoholic drinks were from ours. They did not have things like vodka that could knock you out with one small glass. They did not have cheap and easy access to beer and wine at the supermarket or Circle K. Becoming an alcoholic was unlikely for all but the richest and most powerful people.

What this means is that the Bible's many warnings about alcohol are actually sharper to us today than they were back then. I would say that while there's nothing that doesn't allow you to drink alcohol, you're better off avoiding it anyway.

Read More!

<http://www.tektonics.org/lp/nowine.html>

Chapter 75:

Is Gay Okay?

I'm not an expert on why people are homosexual, so I won't be talking about that here. Instead all I want to do is answer the simple question, *Does the Bible say homosexuality is wrong?* In other words, according to what the Bible says, is gay okay?

What some people will try to do is say that some places where the Bible says homosexuality is wrong, it really means something else. They'll also say that there are places where the Bible shows homosexuals in a positive light. Let's look at five big examples.

#1: Leviticus 18:22. "Do not lie with a man as one lies with a woman; that is detestable." (See also 20:13.) This seems pretty straightforward, but there are some critics who say this has nothing to do with homosexuality itself. Instead, they say, this just doesn't allow homosexual *prostitution.* They also say that the rule was made because it didn't make babies and a man's sperm was considered sacred. Or, they argue that it has to do with pagan religious practices rather than a normal homosexual relationship.

There's a lot of problems with these interpretations. For one thing, this rule is put in with a lot of other rules that also say not to "lie with" your female relatives, like your mother or your aunt, or with animals. There's no way it can be claimed that any of these had to do with things like pagan religious practices. There's also no evidence that the Jews thought that sperm was sacred.

Second, all the later Jewish interpreters of Scripture, and Jewish writers like Philo and Josephus, read these laws as being against homosexuality.

Third, critics have to read things like prostitution *into* the rule. It isn't mentioned. It is specifically mentioned in other places (Deut. 23:17-18) so it's hard to argue that it was just assumed here.

#2: 1 Samuel 18:3-4 "And Jonathan made a covenant with David because he loved him as himself. Jonathan took off the robe he was wearing and gave it to David, along with his tunic, and even his sword, his bow and his belt."

Here's the deal: If you squint real hard and stand on one leg, you *might* see here that David and Jonathan are homosexual partners. It is very hard to find. Critics point out that Jonathan seems to be taking off his clothes, but miss that David apparently isn't. They also don't realize that Jonathan is taking off stuff that signified his royal status – in essence he's giving David his right to the throne.

What about the word "loved"? Well, it's the same word used to say that the Lord loved Israel (Deut.

7:8, 1 Kings 10:9, 2 Chr. 2:11, 9:8, Hosea 3:1), so it doesn't indicate any sort of sexual component.

#3: John 21:21 "Peter turned and saw that the disciple whom Jesus loved was following them. (This was the one who had leaned back against Jesus at the supper and had said, 'Lord, who is going to betray you?')"

On this one, critics like to point out that there was a disciple Jesus "loved" and that he let him lean against him at dinner. Is this a sign of a homosexual relationship? No way. This was actually a very normal way for men in Jesus' culture to interact with each other when they were friends. (If you have ever seen Middle Eastern leaders on the news today, you may have seen them kissing each other on the side of the face. Or maybe you saw the picture of President Bush holding hands with one of the leaders of Saudi Arabia. Those would be examples of the same thing.)

#4: Romans 1:27 "In the same way the men also abandoned natural relations with women and were inflamed with lust for one another. Men committed indecent acts with other men, and received in themselves the due penalty for their perversion."

Just like with Leviticus 18:22, critics will say that this is not addressed to everyday homosexual behavior but to temple prostitution, and non-homosexuals engaging in homosexual sex against their own nature. But once again, this has to be added into the text. It also assumes that people in Paul's time thought homosexuality was something you were "born with," and they didn't. Finally, Paul's words are similar to Jewish condemnations of Gentile wickedness, and there is no evidence that those condemnations were directed at temple prostitution.

#5: 1 Corinthians 6:9 "Do you not know that the wicked will not inherit the kingdom of God? Do not be deceived: Neither the sexually immoral nor idolaters nor adulterers nor male prostitutes nor homosexual offenders...."

The argument made here is that the word translated "homosexual offenders" actually means "effeminate" (meaning, like a woman) or "soft" and therefore refers to people who are cowards, not homosexuals. But the word is clearly used in Greek literature of homosexual men, not of cowards.

Read More!

< http://www.tektonics.org/lp/lev18.html >
<http://www.tektonics.org/qt/romhom.html>

Chapter 76:

Outside Bounds

Sexual temptation is one of the biggest temptations students face in college and young people face as a whole. There's a related temptation to think that sex before marriage isn't sinful. That isn't an option, though, if you're going to use the Bible as a moral guide.

I could throw a lot of Bible verses at you, like Hebrews 13:4: "Marriage should be honored by all, and the marriage bed kept pure, for God will judge the adulterer and all the sexually immoral." There are plenty more where this came from, but instead of using those, I'm going to pull a fast break and use just one more illustration from the Bible that may surprise you.

You probably would miss the book of Hosea if you weren't looking for it, but it has an interesting story that tells us how God views marriage and how important it is (and how important He thinks it is).

It's not too long; you can probably read it in 15 minutes. What you'll find in there is that God looks at sex outside of marriage in *the same way He looks at worshipping a false god*. Why?

Marriage is understood as a *covenant*, or a contract. It is an agreement to devote yourself to one person only. Sex is the most intimate act that can be had between two persons. It brings you close in a way that nothing else can.

If this is so, then it makes sense that it is reserved for people who have committed themselves totally to one another. Without marriage, sex is trivialized. It becomes little more than self-gratification, not an expression of earnest devotion to the other person.

It has to be pointed out that people in Bible times had a simple way to avoid this problem – namely, people got married *very* early, sometimes as early as age 14! That probably wouldn't work too well for us today. But it does tell you how serious they were about avoiding sex outside of marriage. If we can be that serious, then we will find it easier to stay away from it too.

Read More!

<http://www.family.org/faith/A000004320.cfm>

Chapter 77:

The Reincarnation Sensation

These days there are people who argue that the Bible teaches *reincarnation* – the idea that when you die, you can be reborn into another body, maybe another human body, but sometimes an animal's if you didn't do so well in your last life.

There are three arguments most often used by those who claim that the Bible teaches reincarnation as it is now written. (There are also some who say it was removed from the Bible, but they have no evidence for this.) Those arguments are:

Jews in the time of Jesus believed in reincarnation, as documented by the Jewish historian Josephus. This is completely wrong. Josephus says that the Jewish group called the Pharisees believe that "the souls of good men only are removed into other bodies, but that the souls of bad men are subject to eternal punishment." (*War* 2.164) This is contrary to reincarnation principles because it disagrees with the idea of *karma* (see about that below), which holds that bad men get another body of a lower form. Those who use this also misunderstand "other bodies." It refers to *resurrection* bodies, as in Jewish beliefs that men got better and glorified bodies, made from the old molecules of their own body, at the end of history.

There are Scriptures that are difficult to interpret in any way other than that there is a belief in reincarnation. That's not true either. These are the verses:

> Matt. 11:13-14 For all the Prophets and the Law prophesied until John. 14And if you are willing to accept it, he is the Elijah who was to come

It is claimed that this teaches that John was a reincarnation of Elijah. But this would not work because the Old Testament does not teach that Elijah died, but was taken to heaven in a fiery chariot. So Jewish people of Jesus' day believed that Elijah himself would return, not be reincarnated. Anyway, Luke 1:17 makes it clear what this means when it says that John will come in the spirit and power of Elijah, not as Elijah himself.

> Matt. 14:1-2 At that time Herod the tetrarch heard the reports about Jesus, 2and he said to his attendants, "This is John the Baptist; he has risen from the dead! That is why miraculous powers are at work in him."

This could not be reincarnation because Jesus was already alive at the time that John was executed!

The Bible teaches karma: "You will reap what you sow." Then does our justice system operate on karma when it says that "the punishment will fit the crime"? All the essential elements of karma which make it unique missing from the Bible, such as the idea that the reaping is administrated by some cosmic wheel of justice. Gal. 6:7, where this comes from, identifies the personal Jewish God as the agent of retribution.

So there's no way anyone can say that the Bible teaches reincarnation. It requires reading the Bible in a way different than its authors intended.

Read More!

<http://www.tektonics.org/qt/reinc.html>

Chapter 78:

The Perfect Copy

One of the things many Christians believe is that the Bible is the inerrant Word of God. As the leaders of Christianity have defined this, this means we believe that the *original writings* of the Bible were inerrant. We do not think that a modern Bible like the one you read now is inerrant. Only that which was personally written by the authors of the Bible was ever without error, according to this belief. (There are a few Christians who think some versions like the King James Bible are without error, but they're not thought of by most Christians as being right about this.)

But some people ask: *If God is all-powerful, why didn't He make sure all the copies were without error, too?*

The problem with this question is that is makes the assumption that keeping perfect copies around would be a *good* thing. But it isn't.

Hundreds of years ago, the church dealt with a serious problem with what are called *relics*. Relics were claimed to be pieces of Christian history that the average believer could buy, and in exchange not only have it for what it allegedly was, but also perhaps get some favor from God for buying it. Relics were a serious problem partially because people made up fake ones. One saying went that there was enough wood around from the cross of Jesus to build a ship. But regardless of whether they were real or not, many people thought they were real.

Now if this is how allegedly authentic pieces of Christian history were regarded, how would inerrant copies of Scripture have been received? What would happen if each copy had each been inscribed with God's seal and been perfect? The copies themselves would become the most expensive sort of relic, put way out of reach of the common people. Some would have taken to mind to destroy as many copies as they could, and prevent the production of later copies, to increase the value of their own copies. Scribes would be hired to produce (or not produce) more copies for their wealthy customers. This would be the problems of relics a thousand times over.

Have you ever gone to see an exhibit featuring something like the original Declaration of Independence? I did, many years ago, and it was a lot like what you see in the movie *National Treasure*. Visitors were carefully searched before they entered. A maze of pathways led you to the center. There, at the very heart of the exhibit, you could see one of the original copies of the Declaration - inside a glass-topped case that came up on a little sort of elevator, out of a secure area below the observation level.

If this is the type of concern we show for our Declaration of Independence, what would we do with inerrant copies of the Bible? Would we approve of our government, or a church, or some big corporation, hoarding the inerrant copies and guarding them jealously? The Word of God should be accessible to everyone; and if every translation and copy came out inerrant, there would undoubtedly be political, economic or religious powers who would take advantage of the situation, and declare something like that "the common people" had no right or need to have their own copies, just as happened at certain points in Middle Age and pre-Middle Age history.

To those who say that God could or should have taken steps to ensure that every copy and translation was inerrant, I say that if that had been done, the results would have been tragic - far worse than what actually has happened in our history.

Read More!

<http://www.tektonics.org/gk/inerrancy.html>

Chapter 79:

God Breaks the Law

About 300-400 years ago, there were some philosophers who claimed that miracles were impossible. Why?

The argument was that miracles "violated" natural law, and because of this, were impossible. To this day many atheists use this same argument.

But wait a minute. If we lift a box, no one says that this "violates" the law of gravity. So why would it be true that if God lifts a box; is that a "miracle"?

The fact is that the philosophers simply made up a distinction between the acts of men ("natural") and the acts of God, angels, etc. ("supernatural"). There's no such distinction in the Bible, and it is simply made up.

You might say that God does things men can't do, like raise people from the dead. True, but that still doesn't mean these are things we could never do as humans, if we had the right technology, and could use energy the right way.

So to put it in a nutshell, to argue that "miracles are impossible because they violate natural law" is a false argument. If God exists, God can act in the world the same way any human can, and no "law" of any kind can stop Him any more than it can stop us.

Chapter 80:

Never Heard of It!

Some people argue that if God really cared about people, He'd make sure that everyone had a chance to be saved. One person even argued that God could have carved the words "Jesus Lives" on the moon so that everyone would have a testimony of the Resurrection. It's like expecting God to be Batman's butler Alfred, waiting on us hand and foot and maybe issuing some advice now and then (but otherwise, leaving us alone!).

Carving "Jesus Lives" into the moon, or something like that, seems to make sense to us – if only because we already know the Gospel story. But while others are on the way to explain who "Jesus" is (A man? A dog?) and how exactly he "lives" (In a house? As the "life" of the party?), and assuming it was in a language they could understand, others around the world would have time to fill the carving with their own meaning which they would find it hard to give up when missionaries arrive to fill in the details. You could argue that it is better to do without a moon carving or something like that, since there is no chance of a false interpretation that would be harder to get rid of as time passed.

But there's more to it. Being a member of the body of Christ is not just something that starts and stops at conversion but continues throughout life with discipleship and fellowship. A simple carving in the moon won't get you that.

Still, someone may say, "What happens to people who never hear the Gospel? Do they go to hell?" The Bible does not answer this directly, but it gives us clues that provide an answer:

1. The evidence for God is clear, so that men are without excuse (Ps. 19, Rom. 1-2). The heavens already declare God's existence and majesty.
2. He who seeks, finds (Matt. 7:7//Luke 11:9).

The answer to the question, "What about those who never hear the Gospel?" is, "Those who want to know it, will be given the knowledge needed for salvation. Those who seek God will have God sufficiently revealed to them." Notice that it is not lack of hearing the Gospel that causes condemnation; it is *sin* that causes condemnation, and it is not hard to arrive at a conclusion that sin is offensive to whatever powers one may suppose to exist –in fact, the religious history of sacrifice and repentance in religions all around the world throughout history show that people know this! So people have always known that they need help – and these verses tell us that those who look for help will get it.

Chapter 81:

It's Not a Coaster

If you're a Christian, then hopefully your Bible doesn't have a thick coating of dust. But whether it does or it doesn't, there are some good ideas for how to use and read your Bible we'd like to offer. Some today use the Bible as some sort of talisman or even a roulette wheel, in a way that is illustrated by the joke about the man who flipped open a Bible and pointed to a passage as a way of deciding what he should do next with his life: He landed on the passages, "And Judas went and hanged himself" and then, "go ye and do likewise"!

So how about some "do's" and "don'ts" then?

Do:

Memorize texts. If the Bible is the Word of God, or even if it's just an important text in your life, it makes sense to do as you would for any other text you think is important, and memorize important bits of it. Remember, though, just like in your classes in school, it's not enough to just be able to repeat back what you read, but also know what the text *means*. In fact, I'd say that it's far more important to memorize meaning and message than it is to memorize exact words.

Check references. In the book of Acts, the Bereans used the Old Testament to check up on Paul's teachings. This is common sense: If it's the manual for what to believe, you should go and "look it up" when someone makes claims based on it. You should even look up any Bible verses **I** use to make sure I got them right.

Look into context. Some people say you should read the Bible "like a newspaper." That's not fully true. The Bible has books in it in many forms. If you don't know who wrote something in the Bible, and why, it won't speak to you the right way at all. What it boils down to is that you don't show a text respect unless you know what it is saying.

Talk with others on what you read and determine. Iron sharpens iron. If you may be in error, do this for correction; if you are in the right, you will benefit others. This "sharing" also extends to interaction with those in the know about interpretation (commentaries, or at the very least, more than one translation in a pinch).

Read it "Christocentrically". Meaning, more or less, recognize God's overall plan, or take a long view; and avoid such niggling ideas as, "Boy, Old Testament sacrifice sure seemed like a waste of time!"

Examine Yourself. We all bring assumptions to the text, it's a necessary evil (the definitions of English words, for instance). But the dedicated Bible student will, when they read a Bible text that conflicts with their assumptions, revise their assumptions when they are proven wrong.

Do not:

Treat it like a Ouija board. I'm not just talking here about normal reading practice of flipping open just to read, but for the purpose of divining messages from the text, like in the joke at the start of the chapter. I'm not saying God can't speak to you like that (it's obviously *possible* theoretically), but is has no basis in history or precedent. This also goes for when regular reading is done and it is claimed that certain verses "jump out" at you. Perhaps they do — thanks to conscience rather than God. But don't put the jump ahead of the careful step of interpretation and application. The Bible isn't like a telephone God has conversations through. It's more like a letter.

Read it in bite size pieces irrelevant to context. Unless you have some reason to do so, it's not a good idea to divide and read by chapters. The chapters were not in the original, and they only *sometimes* correspond with proper breaks in the story. Look for good narrative or argumentative breaks instead; that is, unless you're one of those sorts of people (and many are) who can easily pick up reading anywhere you have left off without losing track of context.

Feel obliged to read the Bible "in order," or completely over a whole year, etc. Here's some surprising news: *You can limit the amount of time spent reading books like Leviticus and Esther.* These books *should* be read, and understood in their context, but not as often by far as those of more relevance. Go more frequently to more impactful books like Romans.

Force meaning into texts. This is a habit of many modern people who have no concern for original intent of the Biblical authors. If a text's first context does not support a given view, it ought not be used — period.

Chapter 82:

Reading Room

This book, as I said, isn't going to answer every possible argument. No book can do that unless it is big enough to be moved in a fleet of vans. But that's what *one* book can't do. A lot of books – as well as things like websites – put together can answer almost all arguments. I know, since I've read them all. (I mean, the ones you see here. Not all books as in all that have ever existed. I haven't even started on the manga stuff, for example.)

Anyway, here's a list of resources for more information, in case you want to learn more about the topics we've written about here, or are just curious, or even if you want something to make it look like you're reading while you're really asleep on the couch. I've marked books according to what level reader they're for (**B**eginner, **I**n-between, **M**ajor honkin' student) and wrote some notes about some of them, too.

Books

Alcorn, Randy. *Heaven.* **(B)**

Alcorn answers the question, "What is heaven like?" Not bad once you get past the first 50 pages (unless you happen to like anecdotes, then you'll like it all the way through).

Arnold, Clinton. *Zondervan Illustrated Bible Backgrounds Commentary.* **(I)**

Kind of like an encyclopedia which tells you all about background information on the culture and world of the Bible, which in turn can help you understand it better.

Bauckham, Richard. *God Crucified.* **(I)**

Short but heavy book on the divinity of Jesus in the New Testament.

Baukcham, Richard. *Jesus and the Eyewitnesses.* **(M)**

Big, thick book defending the idea that people who actually saw what happened were the ones who wrote the Gospels.

Beckwith, Francis and Greg Koukl. *Relativism: Feet Firmly Planted in Mid-Air* **(B)**

All about the concept of truth vs. pluralism.

Block, Daniel. *Gods of the Nations.* **(M)**
All about concepts of property in the Old Testament. Boring, but helps you understand a lot of the OT better.

Blomberg, Craig. *The Historical Reliability of the Gospels.* **(I)**
Title explains itself.

Bock, Darrell. *Studying the Historical Jesus.* **(I)**
Good for learning about different views of Jesus out there (and what's wrong with most of them).

Bowman, Robert and J. Ed Komoszewski. *Putting Jesus in His Place.* **(B)**
All about the identity and divinity of Jesus in the New Testament.

Boyd, Gregory. *Cynic Sage or Son of God?* **(B)**
All about one view of Jesus as a "cynic".

Boyd, Gregory and Paul Eddy. *The Jesus Legend.* **(I)**
Really honking-useful book that covers a lot of information on studies about Jesus.

Brown, Michael. *Answering Jewish Objections to Jesus.* **(B)**
3 volumes with tons of answers to objections from Jewish critics (which are arguments used by other people too).

Burridge, Richard. *Four Gospels, One Jesus.* **(I)**

About how the Gospels are types of ancient biographies, which helps us understand why they are written as they are.

Carroll, Vincent and David Shiflet. *Christianity on Trial.* **(B)**

About Christianity's positive influence on the world, and against claims that it has been harmful.

Copan, Paul. *True for You But Not For Me.*

Copan, Paul. *Will the Real Jesus Please Stand Up?*

Copan, Paul. *When God Goes to Starbucks.*

Copan's books are useful "grab bags" that deal with important questions.

Craig, William Lane. *Reasonable Faith.* **(B)**

A broad look at evidences for Christianity.

De Silva, David. *Honor, Patronage, Kinship and Purity.* **(I)**

Four important concepts you need to know about to really learn more about the New Testament.

D'Souza, Dinesh. *What's So Great About Christianity?* **(B)**

Another book defending Christianity's positive impact on the world.

Evans, Craig. *Fabricating Jesus.* **(I)**
More on new and strange views of Jesus you might hear about.

Geisler, Norman. *When Critics Ask.* **(B)**

Geisler, Norman. *When Skeptics Ask.* **(B)**
Geisler's books are good starting points for learning. They're grab bags of common questions.

Geivett, R. Douglas. *In Defense of Miracles.* **(I)**
This one defends the idea of miracles mostly from a philosophical view.

Giese, Ronald L. and D. Brent Sandy. *A Guide to Interpreting Old Testament Literary Forms.*
Gives you a better idea how to understand the Old Testament and why it was written the way it was.

Habermas, Gary and Mike Licona. *The Case for the Resurrection of Jesus.* **(B)**
Basic defense of the Resurrection in history.

Hoffmeier, James. *Israel in Egypt.* **(I)**
This one's all about stuff from Genesis and Exodus.

Hurtado, Larry. *The Earliest Christian Artifacts.* **(B)**
All about the physical evidence.

Hurtado, Larry. *Lord Jesus Christ.* **(B)**
More on the claims of the New Testament about Jesus.

Jeffers, James. *The Greco-Roman World of the New Testament Era.* **(B)**
This is another one that offers a lot of useful background information.

Jenkins, Philip. *Hidden Gospels.* **(B)**
About alternative gospel documents, like Thomas and Philip.

Johnston, Philip. *Shades of Sheol.* **(I)**
Specialized book about the Jewish concept of the afterlife.

Kaiser, Walter. *Hard Sayings of the Old Testament.* **(B)**
Like an encyclopedia of Bible questions and answers, for the Old Testament.

Kitchen, Kenneth. *On the Reliability of the Old Testament.* **(B)**
Big, big book that thunders when you open it.

Komoszewski, J. Ed, M. James Sawyer, and Daniel Wallace. *Reinventing Jesus.* **(B)**
Tackles many important questions about the reliability of the New Testament and about Jesus.

Longenecker, Richard. *Biblical Exegesis in the Apostolic Period.* **(M)**

On the ways the New Testament used the Old Testament as prophecies about Jesus.

Malina, Bruce and Jerome Neyrey. *Portraits of Paul.* **(I)**

Actually, it just uses Paul as an example to explain the different way in which ancient people thought, versus modern people; knowing all this is a big help in understanding the Bible.

Malina, Bruce and John Pilch. *Handbook of Biblical Social Values.* **(I)**

Similar to the above, but more like a mini-encyclopedia.

Martin, Dale. *Slavery as Salvation.* **(M)**

About slavery in New Testament times.

Matthews, Victor. *Social World of Ancient Israel.* **(B)**

Cultural handbook for the Old Testament.

Meeks, Wayne. *The First Urban Christians.* **(I)**

Another useful background book.

Moreland. J. P. *Scaling the Secular City.* **(B)**

Another broad introduction to Christian issues of faith.

Pate, C. Marvin. *Communities of the Last Days.* **(B)**
About the people who owned the Dead Sea Scrolls.

Patzia, Arthur. *The Making of the New Testament.* **(B)**
This is on things like the formation of the canon and textual criticism.

Stark, Rodney. *For the Glory of God.* **(B)**
More on Christianity's positive impact.

Stein, Robert. *Playing by the Rules.* **(B)**
Background info on the interpretation of the New Testament.

Strobel, Lee. *The Case for Christ.* **(B)**

Strobel, Lee. *The Case for Faith.* **(B)**

Strobel, Lee. *The Case for Easter.* **(B)**

Strobel, Lee. *The Case for the Real Jesus.* **(B)**
All of Strobel's books are good places to start for defense of your faith. Use them to begin you path to deeper material.

Swinburne, Richard. *The Resurrection of God Incarnate.* **(M)**
Very advanced defense of the Resurrection as historical.

Wenham, David. *Paul: Follower of Jesus or Founder of Christianity?* **(I)**

To answer claims that Paul messed up Christianity.

Wilken, Robert. *The Christians as the Romans Saw Them.* **(B)**

Gives you an idea how offensive Christianity was to ancient people (and so, why it would be hard to believe unless the Resurrection happened).

Wilkins, Michael and J. P. Moreland. *Jesus Under Fire.* **(B)**

Earlier book about different views of Jesus and the reliability of the New Testament.

Witherington, Ben. *The Jesus Quest.* **(B)**

Witherington, Ben. *The Paul Quest.* **(B)**

Witherington is one of my fave authors. Read anything by him you find.

Wright, N. T. *The New Testament and the People of God.* **(M)**

Wright, N. T. *Jesus and the Victory of God.* **(M)**

Wright, N. T. *The Resurrection of the Son of God.* **(M)**

Wright's my other fave author. His books are **huge**! – so make sure you're ready for a steak dinner.

Websites

Tekton Apologetics http://www.tektonics.org

My own website, of course. It has over 1500 articles on a variety of topics.

Christian ThinkTank http://www.christian-thinktank.com

Glenn Miller's website. Not as many articles, but the ones he has are a lot longer and more in depth.

TheologyWeb http://www.theologyweb.com

A forum where I debate critics. I have my own section there, designated by the owners; stop by and see us!

Creation Ministries International http://www.creationministriesinternational.com

For the creation-evolution debate.

Leadership University http://www.leaderu.com

William Lane Craig's website. Strong bent towards philosophical and moral issues.

Apologetics Index http://www.apologeticsindex.com

More of an encyclopedia of links to other sites, and a very good one.

Christian Apologetics and Research Ministry http://www.carm.org

One of the oldest apologetics sites, not as much depth but plenty of topical coverage.

Stand to Reason http://www.str.org

Greg Koukl's apologetics site. Also has a more philosophical bent.

Bede's Library http://www.bede.org.uk

By a friend of mine in the UK. Mostly concerned with historical issues.

Bible.org http://www.bible.org

Not just an online Bible, but a study resource.

Lee Strobel http://www.leestrobel.com

One of the leading communicators in apologetics today.

Christian Research Institute http://www.equip.org

Offers the leading radio show and magazine in apologetics.

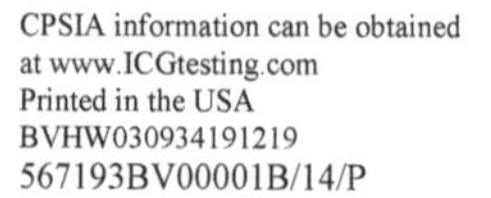

CPSIA information can be obtained
at www.ICGtesting.com
Printed in the USA
BVHW030934191219
567193BV00001B/14/P

9 781606 479919